3 R's for the Gifted

3 R's for the Gifted

Reading, Writing, and Research

Nancy Polette
Assistant Professor of Education
Lindenwood Colleges

1982
Libraries Unlimited, Inc. — Littleton, Colorado

LIBRARIES UNLIMITED, INC.
P.O. Box 263
Littleton, Colorado 80160

Library of Congress Cataloging in Publication Data

Polette, Nancy.
  3 R's for the gifted.

  Includes bibliographies and index.
  1. Gifted children--Education. 2. Creative thinking (Education)   I. Title.
LC3993.2.P63   371.95'3   82-31
ISBN 0-87287-289-0   AACR2

Libraries Unlimited books are bound with Type II nonwoven material that meets and exceeds National Association of State Textbook Administrators' Type II nonwoven material specifications Class A through E.

PREFACE

What is a gifted child? How are school districts throughout the United States identifying candidates for gifted programs? Are classroom teachers prepared to cope with the special education requirements of the gifted? How does an educational program for the gifted child differ from those programs currently offered in the nation's schools? *3 R's for the Gifted* attempts to answer these and numerous other questions concerning gifted education from a practical point of view.

While some educators may disagree that the child most likely to be enrolled in a school district's gifted program is the bright, achieving child, it has been the author's experience that this is, indeed, the child most likely to be found in a gifted program. Programs for the underachieving gifted child do exist, but not to the degree that might be desired. In the many school districts that the author has visited throughout the United States and Canada, educators *are* attempting to adjust and structure programs to meet the needs of more and more children, but established programs for the gifted underachiever are the exception rather than the rule.

An immediate question on the minds of those involved in identifying and working with gifted children who are bright achievers is: "What needs do these children have?" If the child is obviously doing well in school as indicated by both grades and high achievement test scores, isn't the school meeting the needs of these children? *3 R's for the Gifted* attempts to define the very real needs of these students, particularly in the areas of developing productive and critical thinking skills and in providing opportunities for independent pursuit of knowledge often not available to them.

The current state of the art in gifted and talented programs is examined in this book and the bases of defensible educational programs for the gifted student are defined. Among these bases are development of critical and productive thinking skills, which are carefully defined, along with an explanation of numerous strategies that may be employed in their development. This text, then, presents workable curriculum development models and numerous learning modules based on the models.

Creativity is a misunderstood concept among educators and parents alike, the author feels, and attempts in this book to bring theory and practical application together in providing structure for developing the creative process. Few question the need for development of basic skills by all children. The gifted child is no exception. However, when teachers approach the basics from the standpoint of helping the child to become a producer rather than a consumer of knowledge, the child, the school, and ultimately the nation benefit. That is what *3 R's for the Gifted* hopes to help accomplish.

A few words should be said about the organization of this book. Practical classroom exercises included in 12 learning modules make up the bulk of *3 R's for the Gifted*. These modules appear after text material at the end of each chapter. It should be noted, however, that some chapters have sample lessons, exercises, and activities that are included as *part* of text material. These examples have been labeled as figures, and, for easy reference to this material, a list of figures appears at the beginning of the book.

N.P.

ACKNOWLEDGMENTS

The author acknowledges with gratitude the following persons and organizations for their willingness to share their works with others by allowing them to be included in *3 R's for the Gifted*:

Marcella Boerding for her module on fairy tales included in Exploring Fairy Tales.

Constance Cozzoni for her module on animals included in Having Fun with Animals.

Ola Gregory and *Jeanne Brown* for their literature activities included in Going from Reader to Writer.

Ola Gregory for her module about different cultures included in Developing a World View.

Kay Hoffmeister for her module on writing included in Starting with Prewriting Activities and her module about the four seasons included in Studying the Four Seasons.

Suzanne Horn for her module focusing on the works of Beatrix Potter included in Stimulating Reading-Writing Skills.

Celinda Howell for her module about the five senses included in Using the Five Senses.

Carol McKissack for her module dealing with American history included in Building America.

Carla Pund for her module about community helpers included in Learning about Community Helpers.

and

Joyce Juntune, Executive Director of the National Association for Gifted Children, for her extensive contributions to the sections on Bloom's Taxonomy and on Critical and Productive Thinking Skills.

To *Book Lures, Inc.* for permission to include activities from *Super Seven* and from *Book Bogglers*.

TABLE OF CONTENTS

LIST OF ILLUSTRATIONS

1 THE GIFTED AND GIFTED PROGRAMS

The design of educational programs for gifted and talented students is a difficult and challenging process, complicated primarily by the multiplicity of definitions of what constitutes giftedness. In its allocation of funds for gifted programs, the U.S. Office of Education defines gifted and talented children as those:

> identified by professionally qualified persons who by virtue of outstanding abilities are capable of high performance. These are children who require differentiated educational programs and/or services beyond those normally provided by the regular school program in order to realize their contribution to self and society.

> Children capable of high performance include those with demonstrated achievement and/or *potential* ability in any of the following areas, singly or in combination:
>
> 1. general intellectual ability
> 2. specific academic aptitude
> 3. creative or productive thinking
> 4. leadership ability
> 5. visual and performing arts
> 6. psychomotor ability*

A realistic appraisal of this list of abilities leads many educators to the conclusion that almost every child in U.S. schools today would qualify for specialized instruction in at least one area. To complicate the problem, the rise in interest in education of the gifted is occurring in an educational age emphasizing accountability, competency testing, and "back to the basics." It is little wonder that educators are in a quandary, knowing that schools will be held accountable for all educational programs including those that attempt to identify and provide a differentiated form of instruction for gifted students.

IDENTIFICATION OF THE GIFTED

The solution to the problem in most school districts has been to rely heavily on objective criteria in the identification process. Often this process includes selection of students who 1) score at the 95th percentile or above on standardized

---

*Sidney P. Marland, Jr. Education of the Gifted and Talented vol. 1, Report to the Congress of the United States by the U.S. Commissioner of Education (Washington, DC), Government Printing Office, 1972.

achievement tests; 2) score in the top three to five percent on individualized intelligence tests, usually indicating an IQ of 125 or above; 3) are recommended by their teachers or peers for participation in such a program; or 4) receive high scores on tests of creativity. High scores on three out of four measures are usually required. Application of the above criteria is *not* universal, but its practice is common enough to indicate that the majority of students identified for participation in gifted programs fall within that U.S. Office of Education gifted identification area known as *academic aptitude.* In other words, many of the nation's gifted programs are populated by bright, motivated youngsters who are doing well in school.

While a case might be made for differentiated educational programs to meet the needs of high IQ children who are *not* performing in line with their abilities, or for students who show creative rather than academic talent (both who may be in remedial programs), few school districts have the resources to provide for *these* gifted children other than in the remedial programs where many of them are currently placed.

There are exceptions to this, however. Educators are watching with interest the development of such pioneer programs as the counseling programs for intellectually gifted students in Kent and Seattle, Washington; the primary programs for culturally different potentially gifted students in Albuquerque, New Mexico; IEP programs in Omaha, Nebraska and Wheeling, West Virginia; leadership development programs in Waterloo, Iowa and Alice, Texas; and fine arts, visual arts and performing arts programs in Birmingham, Alabama, Concord, New Hampshire, and St. Louis, Missouri. These and similar programs have, on the one hand, been praised for their sincere efforts in attempting to meet the needs of children with a particular type of giftedness, and, on the other hand, pressured to expand their gifted programs to serve children who may be gifted in other areas. Most school districts, therefore, have opted to include as many students as possible in their gifted programs through relying heavily on identification of the *academically talented* student.

Among the best of these programs, sincere efforts have been made in defining the special needs of these children and in providing a program structure in which **every child in the school benefits in some way** from the school's gifted program. The most common characteristic of *these* programs is the cluster grouping of intellectually gifted and academically talented students within the normal classroom. The teacher of this gifted/normal class:

1. has made a commitment to becoming a highly trained gifted educator;

2. has played a major role in curriculum development for the gifted program;

3. undergoes periodic in-service training to keep abreast of the best that is known today about teaching gifted children;

4. understands that all children are unique and that each child in his or her class has special abilities or talents which must be nurtured.*

---

*For a listing and brief description of successful cluster group programs, see *Successful Programs for the Gifted and Talented*, edited by Joyce Juntune. National Association for Gifted Children, 1981.

A major question that arises when planning instruction for a gifted class, most of whose members are bright children doing well in school, is that of determining the specific needs of these children that are *not* being met in the regular academic program. An examination of criteria for admission to the program not only helps define these specific needs, but points the way for development of a curriculum that *will* have an impact on *all* children in the school.

Of all criteria used in identification of the gifted, the standardized achievement test probably carries the most weight. Few teachers would agree that a sixth-grader reading on a second-grade level (even though his or her IQ may be 140) should be admitted to a gifted program, even though this child may be most in need of a differentiated instructional program. By their very nature, standardized achievement tests are objective, convergent, and content-oriented. The child who memorizes well and easily acquires basic skills in reading, mathematics, and composition, does well on these tests. This is the child who is comfortable with convergent (one right answer) questions and whose world is concrete rather than abstract. This is the child who has learned to **respond** rather than to **think**, and here lies the clue to the most basic need of these children – a curriculum, divergent in nature, that teaches children to think!

When a program designed to make children think is initiated, particularly in a gifted/normal cluster group classroom, teachers often discover that the most unique and original responses come from children who are *not* a part of the gifted cluster group. Children within the gifted group are often challenged into new areas of thought by their less academically talented peers. On the other hand, those children who do need help in acquisition of basic content and skills are often more highly motivated to acquire these skills when emphasis in instruction shifts from **content** to **process** and **product.** This does not mean a departure from teaching the basics, but a different approach to the basics, one which values each student as a **producer** of knowledge rather than as a **consumer.**

BASIC PREMISES OF GIFTED EDUCATION

Three basic characteristics of a differentiated educational program for gifted students are cited in the Marland Report referred to earlier:

1. A differentiated curriculum which denotes higher cognitive concepts and processes.

2. Instructional strategies which accommodate the learning styles of the gifted and talented and curriculum content.

3. Special grouping arrangements which include a variety of administrative procedures appropriate to particular children, i.e., special classes, honor classes, seminars, resource rooms and the like.

In addition, other considerations in the development of curriculum, materials, and instructional strategies for the gifted include:

1. Emphasis on process and product rather than content;

2. Emphasis on the developmental thinking processes of early childhood;

3. Emphasis on productive thinking skills (fluency, flexibility, originality, elaboration);

4. Emphasis on critical thinking skills (planning, forecasting, problem-solving, decision-making, and evaluation);

5. Investigation of real problems and situations;

6. Emphasis on acquisition of skills for the independent pursuit of knowledge;

7. Use of resources beyond the school.

A misconception often occurs in examining this list of elements in gifted education. The question arises, once again, over the absence of any reference to "the basics." However, any process-oriented program must rely heavily on the basics of reading, writing, and research to be successful. An original composition cannot be written and communicated to others without competent use of spelling, grammar, and sentence and paragraph construction. Investigation of any problem requires a search for reliable data encompassing both research and reading skills before the student can support or deny existing concepts and develop new concepts through the use of a wide variety of carriers of knowledge. The very concept of **product** implies a high level of competence in basic skills and considerable understanding of basic concepts.

As evolution of gifted education continues, we see emerging programs that will ultimately benefit *all* children. These are programs that are functional in nature, blending the necessary acquisition of basic skills with instructional strategies designed to teach children to think, to create, and to value themselves and their unique contributions to the society of which they are a part.

3 R's for the Gifted is intended as a help to teachers seeking better methods for working with gifted children and with all children. The book provides curriculum design strategies that blend higher-level thinking processes with basic skills instruction and includes actual learning modules in areas of reading, writing, and research that can be adapted for use in many types of instructional programs.

The goal of American education has always been to help children reach their full potential as contributing members of a free society. The strategies developed for use in gifted programs may well provide the means for meeting this goal with all children.

DESIGNING CURRICULUM FOR GIFTED PROGRAMS

A major misconception that arises when considering a curriculum for gifted students is that no basic instruction is needed since gifted/academically talented students learn easily on their own. Thus, changes in curriculum for these children often include additional assignments, acceleration, or independent study programs. The focus of curriculum change in these programs is on enrichment rather than gifted education.

Newer curriculum designs based on the work of Guilford/Meeker, Renzulli, Williams, Moffat, Torrance, and Terman combine an emphasis on process and product with a structured approach to helping children acquire higher-level thinking skills. With this in mind, the following 15 components would be found in a language arts (reading, writing, and research) program for gifted students:

1. Emphasis on **process** rather than **content**

2. Emphasis on **product**

3. Emphasis on the higher cognitive levels of Bloom's taxonomy (see chapter 2): Application, Analysis, Syntheses, Evaluation

4. Development of critical reading skills and critical judgment

5. Expanded vocabulary development

6. Development of literature skills and understanding

7. Emphasis on **productive thinking skills**: Fluency, Flexibility, Originality, Elaboration

8. Emphasis on **critical thinking skills**: Planning, Forecasting, Decision-Making, Problem-Solving, Evaluation

9. Use of resources *beyond* the classroom and the school

10. Exposure to a wide range of **imaginative** literature

11. Development of skills in visual literacy

12. Assured competency in basic research skills, including: Location, Acquisition, Organization, Recording, Evaluation, Verification

13. Planned experiences for younger children in development of Piaget's cognitive tasks (see chapter 2): Conservation, Seriation, Classification, Reversibility

14. Planned experiences for older children in exploration of values through literature

15. A high level of skills competency in reading, writing, speaking, listening, research, and all related communication skills

In development of such a curriculum, the following steps should be considered:

1. Define long-range goals — What skills and concepts should children permanently acquire?

2. Define intermediate objectives — What skills and concepts do we want children to be exposed to this year?

3. Develop a concept hierarchy for material to be covered over a specific length of time (see Fig. 1-1, page 18).

4. Match content and process (see Fig. 1-2, page 19).

5. Determine evaluation procedures, both formative and summative.

Figure 1-1
Hierarchy of Selected Literature Concepts

Time Period: Six-Week Module

Plot	Character	Setting	Theme
Recalls major events in order	Identifies character development through—character's actions, speech, thoughts,	Recognizes elements of setting—time, place	Understands four universal themes used in literature
Recognizes contrived plot and inconsistencies	what others say about character, other's actions toward character	Relates elements of setting to plot	Identifies story elements related to theme
Understands relationship of plot, character, setting, and mood	Recognizes stereotypes	Recognizes relationship of character's actions and moods to setting	Identifies relation of title to theme

Figure 1-2
Literature Concepts and Processes

Productive Thinking	Critical Thinking	Research
Name as many magic objects from folk tales as you can—how is each important to the plot of the tale?	You are now the size of The Borrower's. How will this change your life?	Research the lives of Davy Crockett or Daniel Boone. Did either man actually perform all of the feats attributed to him? Support your answer.
Greed is a major theme of *A Christmas Carol*. Name other famous tales with this same theme.	Why didn't Pippi Longstocking go to school every day like other nine-year-olds?	One universal theme is good versus evil. Visit your library and find as many tales as you can that have this theme.
Develop a card game requiring the players to match characters with settings in well-known tales.	In Peter Pan both Indians and Pirates are found in Never Never Land. Change these to other groups of people. How would the story change?	A film company is looking for a country ideal for filming *The Hobbit*. Where would you send them and why?
Name characters from literature who are associated with particular character traits. Ex.: Scrooge—stinginess.	If Mary Poppins lost her umbrella, what object could replace it and still be in keeping with her character?	Compare the Greek and Roman Gods—chart the powers of each. Which Gods have similar powers?

2 THINKING SKILLS: WHAT ARE THEY?

An examination of a typical teacher's manual for most disciplines reveals an emphasis on the acquisition of content and test questions that are convergent in nature. Instruction is centered around the three lowest levels of cognitive development: knowledge, comprehension, and application. Teachers have long held that if a child can repeat an answer, understand the concept or skill, and apply it, then instruction is successful. Research indicates that in most classrooms, 70% to 80% of instructional time is spent in these three lower-thinking skill areas. On the other hand, programs in gifted education are more concerned with the higher-level thinking processes of analysis, synthesis, and evaluation. A review of these levels of thinking provides a more complete explanation of each level.

BLOOM'S TAXONOMY

Educator Benjamin S. Bloom in 1956 developed a taxonomy of educational objectives that is still used today. The following outline was compiled by Joyce Juntune, Executive Director of the National Association for Gifted Children, and is based on Bloom's *Taxonomy of Educational Objectives: The Classification of Educational Goals, Handbook I: Cognitive Domain.* (© 1956 by Longman Inc.) (The outline is used with permission of Joyce Juntune.)

Levels of Thinking

I. **Knowledge**

In the Taxonomy, **Knowledge** refers to the ability to recognize or recall information. It should not be confused with a philosophical definition. Teaching this phase of the Taxonomy merely involves "pouring in" information. This phase of instruction is usually accomplished in a formal setting. It can be accomplished with large groups.

   A. Activities usually done by student:
   1. Responds to classroom situation — is attentive
   2. Absorbs information — looks, listens, reads
   3. Remembers
   4. Practices affective procedures — drills, recites
   5. Covers information in books
   6. Recognizes information that has been covered

B. Evidence of student's success:
1. Completes class and homework assignments
2. Completes programmed learning sequences
3. Scores satisfactorily on objective tests

C. Activities usually done by teacher:
1. Directs student activities
2. Gives information—lectures, drills
3. Shows information—audiovisuals, demonstrations
4. Enlarges information
5. Makes and administers objective tests
6. Makes homework assignments

II. Comprehension

Comprehension represents the second lowest level of understanding. The student should be able to make some use of the knowledge that he/she has gained, but he/she may not necessarily be able to relate it to other material or see its fullest implications. This instruction is usually accomplished in a formal setting with a group no larger than a typical class.

A. Activities usually done by student:
1. Explains information rather than merely quotes it
2. Makes simple demonstrations
3. Translates information into his/her own words
4. Extends information to new situations
5. Interprets information from technical terms to familiar terms

B. Evidence of student's success:
1. Has the ability to intelligently discuss information
2. Can write simple essay
3. Scores satisfactorily on objective tests

C. Activities usually done by teacher:
1. Demonstrates material
2. Listens to students
3. Asks questions
4. Compares and contrasts student's answers
5. Examines student's ideas
6. Makes and administers objective tests and low-level essay tests
7. Makes carefully selected homework assignments

III. Application

Application refers to the ability to use abstractions in particular and concrete situations. An example of this phase could be using an abstract mathematical formula to solve a specific math problem. In this phase, instruction is usually rather informal. It is readily adaptable to laboratories, shops, the field, the stage, or to small groups within the classroom.

A. Activities usually done by student:
1. Solves novel problems
2. Constructs projects, models, apparatus, etc.
3. Demonstrates use of knowledge

B. Evidence of student's success:
   1. Masters problem-solving tests
   2. Constructs equipment, models, graphs, etc.
   3. Demonstrates ability to use equipment

C. Activities usually done by teacher:
   1. Shows student ways to facilitate his/her work
   2. Observes student's activities
   3. Criticizes student's activities
   4. Helps design student's projects
   5. Organizes field trips and contests

IV. **Analysis** (More appropriate in gifted education)

Analysis refers to the breaking down of a communication into its basic parts. This allows relationships among ideas to be seen more clearly and allows basic arrangements to be studied. This phase of instruction is best conducted in an informal and irregular manner. Small group and independent study techniques are especially useful here. Homework assignments directed toward analysis are especially valuable.

A. Activities usually done by students:
   1. Discusses information in depth
   2. Uncovers interrelationships among ideas
   3. Discovers deeper meanings and insinuations not apparent at first
   4. Sees similarities and differences between styles

B. Evidence of student's success:
   1. Makes effective outlines
   2. Writes effective précis
   3. Completes effective experimental write-ups

C. Activities usually done by teacher:
   1. Probes, guides, and observes student
   2. Acts as a resource person
   3. Plans for and conducts discussions, seminars, and group critiques

V. **Synthesis**

Synthesis is the putting together of elements or parts to form a whole. It is the arranging and combining of pieces to form a pattern or structure that was not clearly evident before. This phase of the Taxonomy is especially adaptable to independent study. It can be accomplished in almost any setting, including the home. The library is especially useful. Much reflection is generally required — these results often come slowly. Patience is necessary.

A. Activities usually done by student:
   1. Produces unique communications
   2. Formulates new hypotheses based on analyzed information
   3. Makes discoveries and generalizations
   4. Shows relationships between ideas and philosophies
   5. Proposes new ways of doing things

    B.   Evidence of student's success:
        1.   Activities above are effectively completed
        2.   Writes quality essays and term papers
        3.   Makes blueprints or sets of plans for projects

    C.   Activities usually done by teacher:
        1.   Extends student's knowledge
        2.   Analyzes and evaluates student's work
        3.   Prepares reading lists — including critical questions
        4.   Brings in consultants
        5.   Plans seminars
        6.   Allows for independent study

Process Verbs Used for Stating Learning Objectives According to Bloom

1. KNOWLEDGE		This is mainly learning the information.		
define	repeat	list	memorize	name
label	record	recall	relate	

2. COMPREHENSION		Student has to have some knowledge. The difference here is that the student is required to restate information in his/her own way.		
restate	describe	explain	identify	report
discuss	recognize	express	locate	review

3. APPLICATION		This mainly requires the student to explain.		
translate	apply	employ	practice	demonstrate
interpret	operate	schedule	illustrate	dramatize

4. ANALYSIS		This mainly requires the student to break down information into parts.		
distinguish	debate	question	solve	differentiate
compare	diagram	inventory	contract	experiment
test	analyze	criticize	relate	calculate

5. SYNTHESIS		The student produces something new and different of his/her own.		
compose	propose	formulate	assemble	construct
design	arrange	collect	organize	prepare

6. EVALUATION		The student judges the value of information. This is the highest level — contains elements of all the previous levels.		
judge	compare	choose	estimate	evaluate
score	predict	rate	value	assess
select	measure			

In planning instruction using higher-level thinking processes, selection of specific process verbs found at those levels can be most helpful. For example, assume that as a part of the reading lesson a second-grade class has read *Rumplestiltskin*, typical teacher questions might be content-oriented, while those of the teacher of gifted are product-oriented.

C
O
N   1.   **Name** the characters in the story (knowledge).
T
E   2.   **Identify** the good characters and the bad characters (comprehension).
N
T   3.   Act out a scene from the story that **describes** how Rumplestiltskin felt
      when he was cheated (application).

P   4.   **Debate** — Rumplestiltskin was really a good character (analysis).
R
O   5.   **Compose** a poem describing a character or scene from the story
D   (synthesis).
U
C   6.   Of all the fairy tales we have read, **choose** the one you liked best.
T
      Give three reasons for your choice (evaluation).

PIAGET'S CLASSIFICATION

The *level* of questions used has no relation to the age of the child. Very young children *can* make comparisons, compose and design, solve problems, and make judgments centered around *concrete* experiences. However, in gifted programs for preschool and primary children, development of the thinking processes of early childhood must also be considered. The definition of these processes arises from the developmental theories of Jean Piaget:

The Developmental Thinking Processes of Early Childhood (Piaget)

A.   Classification: The ability to group items through identification of one or more common elements and the ability to relate parts to the whole

This skill can be demonstrated when children:
1.   Work jigsaw puzzles
2.   Find the main idea in a story
3.   Group objects by common element (ex. all red things, all soft things)
4.   Compose descriptive titles for pictures or stories

B.   Seriation: the ability to sequence objects or events, to follow directions by performing tasks in the order given

Children demonstrate this skill when they:
1.   Arrange objects in sequential order, i.e., largest to smallest or first to last

    2. Retell events in a story in correct order

C. Conservation: the ability to see that an object remains the same regardless of change in size, shape, or arrangement

The child who conserves is able to:
1. Recognize that a letter can be either upper- or lower-case
2. Recognize equal groups even though objects within a group may be rearranged

D. Reversibility: the ability to follow a line of thought back to its beginning

The child who has achieved reversibility of thought is able to:
1. Recount story events in reverse order
2. Do simple subtraction problems
3. Retrace his own steps or actions in order

Books on Thinking Processes

While these developmental thought processes of early childhood cannot be taught directly, young children need many opportunities to meet these processes. Some of the best of these opportunities occur when the teacher orally shares delightful picture books. Note the thinking processes called for in each of these titles:

Balian, Lorna. *The Humbug Witch.* (Abingdon, 1970).

The tiny witch was truly ferocious! She had a long nose, stringy hair, a black hat and a cat named Fred. But none of her spells would work. Finally, she decided to give up. Off came the stringy red hair, the black hat and the mask with its ugly long nose and teeth, and under all of that was a little girl who went to bed.
(seriation, conservation)

Charlip, Remy. *Hooray for Me!* (Four Winds, 1980).

Here is a tale of countless children, all celebrating their selfhood. "I am my big sister's baby brother." "I am my dog's walker." "We are this book's readers." A delightful exercise in ...
(classification)

Elting, Mary. *Q Is for Duck.* (Houghton Mifflin, 1980).

An alphabet guessing game asks, Why is Q for duck? Because a duck quacks, of course. Children will discover, too, why A is for zoo and E is for whale as they receive more practice in ...
(classification)

Hill, Donna. *Mr. Peeknuff's Tiny People.* (Atheneum, 1981).

To Mr. Peeknuff, who lives high on a hill, everything below is tiny. He liked watching the tiny people below until one day a terrible wind created all kinds of disasters. Mr. P hurried down the mountain to help but could not find any of the tiny people he had been watching. There were only big people like himself. He never found out where his tiny people were!
(conservation)

Kalan, Robert. *Blue Sea*. (Greenwillow, 1979).

A little fish swims away from big fish; they swim away from bigger fish and all swim away from the biggest fish. They swim through successively smaller holes until there is only one little fish left in his blue sea. Introduction of two thought processes ...
(seriation, reversibility)

Other recent titles useful in either assisting in the development of, or identifying the level of, thinking in the young child are:

Cognitive Development: Early Childhood Conservation (C); Seriation (S); Classification (CL); Reversibility (R)

Anno, Mitsumasa. *Anno's Counting Book*. Illus. by the author. (Crowell, 1975). (S) and (CL)

Balian, Lorna. *The Aminal*. (Abingdon, 1972). (S) and (CL)

Balian, Lorna. *The Humbug Witch*. (Abingdon, 1970). (C)

Barrett, Judi. *Animals Should Definitely Not Act Like People*. Illus. by Ron Barrett. (Atheneum, 1980). (R)

Bonsall, Crosby. *Who's Afraid of the Dark?* Illus. by the author. (Greenwillow, 1980). (R)

Brown, Marcia. *Once a Mouse*. (Fable from India). (Charles Scribner's Sons, 1961). (K-2) (C) and (R)

Carle, Eric. *Twelve Tales from Aesop*. (Philomel, 1980). (C)

Charlip, Remy, and Moore, Lilian. *Hooray for Me!* Illus. by Vera B. Williams. (Originally from Parents Magazine Press. Reissued by Four Winds, 1980). (CL)

Elting, Mary, and Folsom, Michael. *Q Is for Duck*. Illus. by Jack Kent. (Houghton Mifflin/Clarion, 1980). (CL)

Hill, Donna. *Mr. Peeknuff's Tiny People*. Illus. by Alan Daniel. (Atheneum, 1981). (C)

Janosch. *Hey, Presto! You're a Bear!* Illus. by the author. An Atlantic Monthly Press Book. (Little, 1977). (R)

Kahl, Virginia. *Whose Cat Is That?* Illus. by the author. (Charles Scribner's Sons, 1979). (C)

Kalan, Robert. *Blue Sea*. Illus. by the author. (Greenwillow, 1979). (S)

Lionni, Leo. *The Greentail Mouse*. Illus. by the author. (Pantheon, 1973). (C)

Lobel, Arnold. *A Treeful of Pigs*. Illus. by Anita Lobel. (Greenwillow, 1979). (R)

Marzollo, Jean. *Close Your Eyes*. Illus. by Susan Jeffers. (Dial, 1978). (R)

Mathews, Louise. *The Great Take-Away*. Illus. by Jeni Bassett. (Dodd, 1980). (R)

Nobel, Trinka Hakes. *The Day Jimmy's Boa Ate the Wash*. Illus. by Steven Kellogg. (Dial, 1980). (R)

Saunders, Susan. *Wales' Tale*. Illus. by Marilyn Hirsch. (Viking, 1980). (R)

Worth, Valerie. *Curlicues. The Fortunes of Two Pug Dogs*. Illus. by Natalie Babbitt. (Farrar, Straus & Giroux, 1980). (R)

Yolen, Jane. *All in the Woodland Early*. Illus. by Jane Zalben. (Collins, 1979). (CL)

PRODUCTIVE AND CRITICAL THINKING SKILLS

Among the most frequently used strategies in gifted programs are those based on the goal of developing productive and critical thinking skills with students. It is an organized approach to stimulate a variety of ways of thinking and to help children use both present and future knowledge.

When classes become adept in fluency, planning, decision-making, or problem-solving, teachers often see unused potential begin to emerge among individual students. In combining theory and practice with the "why" of learning stressed through critical and productive thinking skills, teachers *are* able to stress the basics and beyond in classrooms that have a whole different atmosphere.

The summary of skills and warm-up activities included here were adapted by Joyce Juntune, Executive Director, National Association for Gifted Children. The following outline is included here to assist readers in future reference.

I. Productive Thinking
   A. Fluency
   B. Flexibility
   C. Originality
   D. Elaboration

II. Critical Thinking
   A. Planning
   B. Communication
      1. Description within categories
      2. Description of feelings
      3. Comparisons and relationships
      4. Empathy
      5. Nonverbal communication
      6. Composition
      7. Sample warm-ups
   C. Forecasting
   D. Decision-Making
   E. Evaluation
   F. Summary

III. Creative Problem-Solving
   A. Fact-Finding
   B. Problem-Finding
   C. Idea-Finding
   D. Solution-Finding

I. **Productive Thinking** is thinking of as many solutions as possible to a given problem. The kinds of productive thinking are:

A. **Fluency** is the ability to produce usually common responses to a given situation. The emphasis is on quantity rather than quality.

1. The first responses are usually common responses.

2. During a session of brainstorming, the best ideas come in the last 25% of the ideas given.

3. Teachers should try to keep the flow going by:
    a) looking for different ideas;
    b) encouraging "hitchhiking" (getting an idea from someone else);
    c) deferring judgment—this is especially difficult for teachers, but the flow will not continue if the student waits to see if the idea is liked.

4. Hypnotism has shown that there are many, many more ideas waiting in the subconscious.

5. An accepting atmosphere must be provided.

6. Writing answers can limit children's ability.

7. One way of achieving fluency is to have children work in pairs, having first one child talk on a particular subject and then switch to the other child and let him/her continue on the same subject.

8. Sample warm-ups:
    a) "List as many red things as you can."
    b) "List all the things you can think of that are hollow."
    c) "List as many compound words as you can."
    d) "List as many three-syllable words as you can."

B. **Flexibility** is the ability to respond in a variety of categories. Flexibility is important because thinking can get stuck on one subject. It is explained to children in this way.

1. It is compared to a department store spending spree. Ten dollars may be spent. Only one item may be purchased in each department. What items could be purchased?

2. Another comparison is with a magic show. Teacher withdraws an imaginary item from a hat. Children name item and continue to name items as long as they are from a different category. If a category is repeated, the game ends.

3. Another comparison is a fishing trip. Each fish that is reeled in is named. When categories are repeated, trip ends.

Children in kindergarten and first grade can understand the concept of flexibility when presented in these terms.

4. Sample warm-ups:
    a) "Categorize the red things you listed in the sample warm-up Fluency activity 8.a. How many categories do you have?"
    b) "Look at your list of three-syllable words. (Fluency 8.d.). How many of you listed foods? Animals? Furniture? What other categories could we use? How many categories did you have?"

c) "What different items could you buy in a large discount store?" (encourage items from many departments).

d) "You are helping your parents clean the garage. What different things might you find?"

C. **Originality** is the ability to make clever, unique responses. There are two kinds of originality:

1. Ideas original to society.

2. Ideas original to this group at this particular time and place.

   a) A child should not sit forever on the ownership of an idea;

   b) Once an idea is out, it forces the child to think of another;

   c) One strategy is to work with books—choose one that offers several ideas—ask children to extend ideas and try to come up with original ideas.

3. Sample warm-ups:

   a) "What red item (Fluency 8.a.) did you list that you think no one else listed?"

   b) "What three-syllable word do you think is your most unusual?" (Fluency 8.d.).

   c) "What could we do with this table so it would be used differently from any other table in the school?"

   d) "What new idea could our class use to make money?"

D. **Elaboration** is expanding a basic idea to make it more interesting and complete.

1. It is taking what you want to get done and making it clear enough so that it can get done.

2. One exercise to follow after brainstorming for nouns and verbs is to write a sentence using one of the nouns. Then cross out the word and add two words in its place. Continue this process, but stay with the original subject. A teacher can roam the room during this time and set standards for different children according to their abilities.

3. Sample warm-ups:

   a) "Choose a three-syllable word from your list. (Fluency 8.d.). How could you elaborate on that word?" (Story? Sentence? Picture? Song?)

   b) Hold up a dictionary. "How could we elaborate on this cover to make it more interesting and attractive?"

   c) Draw a circle on the board. "Who will come to the board and elaborate on this shape to change its appearance)" (allow children to come up in turn and add to each other's ideas).

II. **Critical Thinking** is thinking that encompasses the three higher levels of Bloom's Cognitive Taxonomy: analysis, synthesis, and evaluation. The major critical thinking processes are planning, forecasting, problem-solving, decision-making, and evaluation.

A. **Planning** is organizing a method for achieving a specific solution or outcome. The planning process includes the following steps:

1. Identification—the teacher helps the student state what he/she wants to do (problem or project) with enough additional information to explain what he/she plans to accomplish. Decision-making precedes this step.
2. Materials—the teacher assists the student in listing materials necessary to carry out the project.
3. Steps—the teacher assists the child in looking at all steps involved in actually carrying out his/her play. Organization of materials, time, and resources must be included.
   a) The first task is usually gathering materials—children should make reference to all materials;
   b) Last step is clean-up.
4. Problems—the teacher leads the student to consider problems he/she might encounter.
   a) It is difficult to get flexibility here;
   b) Lack of supplies does not constitute a legitimate problem—should not be planning a project for which no supplies are available.

   Plans may include ideas that may not be able to be actually carried out (such as, "Make a rock"), or they may be plans that are intended to be carried out. (Fig. 2-1, page 30, is a sample work sheet that may be used in the planning process.)
5. Sample warm-ups:
   a) "If I were to make lemonade, what materials would I need? What steps would I follow? What different kinds of problems might I have?" (allow for response after each step).
   b) "My pet needs a bath. Let's plan how we will proceed. What problems might we have?" (allow for response after each step).
B. **Communication** is the ability to express thoughts and ideas to others and includes the following areas:
   1. Description within categories—the teacher encourages the student to list many words within given categories.
      a) Set categories;
      b) List words;
      c) Combine words to write phrases, sentences, stories, poetry, etc.
   2. Description of feelings—the teacher encourages the student to use a variety of words to describe his/her feelings and values.
      a) Use empathy situations as they arise in classroom rather than trying to invent situations;
      b. Use pictures of moods and emotions.
   3. Comparisons and relationships—the teacher leads students to make comparisons among things or to show relationships and associations.
      a) It's good for the student to bring two things together for comparison;

Figure 2-1
Planning Work Sheet

NAME _____   PLANNING

WORK SHEET

I am going to: _____

_____

The things I will need are:

_____
_____
_____

The steps I will take are:

_____
_____
_____

Problems I might have are:

_____
_____
_____

      b)   He/she asks how they are alike and how they are different;
      c)   Then he/she determines how they might be put together.
  4.   Empathy—the teacher builds upon opportunities for students to share personal experiences or thoughts that are similar to the experiences or thoughts of others.
      a)   This is a spontaneous situation;
      b)   It is verbally recognized when observed in students;
      c)   It cannot be preplanned.
  5.   Nonverbal communication—the teacher guides the student to become more skillful in interpreting and using nonverbal forms of communication to express his/her feelings, thoughts, and needs to others. These are progressive stages:
      a)   Throw out words and ask children to react with whole body;
      b)   Give situations and ask children to react;
      c)   List occupations or categories and ask children to strike pose of one and then freeze;
      d)   Create a circumstance and tell children to play a scene in small groups without discussing it with anyone—just look around and find a way to fit in;
      e)   Portray an idea using a symbol.
  6.   Composition—the teacher creates opportunities for the student to organize words into meaningful networks of meanings, thoughts, and needs.

      Questioning—the teacher asks questions about details, but stays centered on the subject.

7. Sample warm-ups:
   a) Description within given categories—"One part of communication is using descriptive words. Let's look at this snowball. What words describe how it looks? What words describe how it feels?"
   b) Description of feelings—"Describe how you feel when you've called all your friends. Accurately describe your feelings."
   c) Comparison/Relationships—Give each student a cotton ball. "What words can you use to finish the sentence: Cotton is as white as ... "
   d) Empathy—Empathy does not lend itself to written activity. It is most effectively developed when it is positively reinforced as it occurs in the classroom.
   e) Composition—"Yesterday the mailman came to my house with a gigantic package addressed to me. Then what do you think happened?"

      "Suppose you came to class one day and found a substitute teacher and no directions to follow. Compose, in your own mind, what you would need to tell him/her. Be sure your ideas are expressed clearly and concisely." Have the students orally give directions as they would give them to the substitute.
   f) Nonverbal acting out—"Show me, using your face, how you feel when you eat a foot-long hot dog. Add your hands and body to help show. Now pretend you have had 35 hot dogs! Show how you feel."

C. **Forecasting** is the ability to predict many different causes and/or effects of a given situation. Forecasting includes the following steps:
   1. The student considers all possible causes and results for a given situation. The student should think in terms of cause and effect. The form in Fig. 2-2, page 32, may be used. The cause does not have to be related to the effect.
      a) One area (cause or effect) may be worked on at one time. Tell children you are only using part of the process.
      b) The guideline to be used in forecasting is flexibility. When you begin to think along category lines, you are able to get your mind out of a rut.
   2. The student examines the quality of each prediction.
   3. The student chooses his/her best cause and/or best effect.
   4. The student gives reasons for his/her choice. The ability to follow this process in forecasting carries over in determining behavior.

Figure 2-2
Forecasting Form

Situational Statement

Causes	Effects (Results)

5. Sample warm-ups:
    a) "I lost a dime. What caused me to lose it? What effects might this have? Choose the most interesting cause and effect. Defend your choices with at least three reasons."
    b) "It snowed popcorn last night. What are all the reasons for this (cause)? What are all the things that will happen because it snowed popcorn (effects)? Choose the best cause and effect. Defend your choices with at least three reasons."
D. **Decision-Making** follows the following steps:
    1. Alternatives—the teacher encourages the student to think of many alternatives to a problem he/she wishes to solve.
    2. Criteria—the teacher assists the student in establishing criteria for weighing each alternative.
    3. Weighing—the teacher assists the student in weighing his/her alternatives in terms of his/her criteria. The following grid may be used for this purpose.

Figure 2-3
Grid Used in Weighing

Alternative
Alternative
Alternative
Alternative

4. Judgment—the teacher guides the student in eliminating some of the alternatives and encourages him/her to make a simple judgment, choice, or decision.
    a) The top choice on the criteria chart does not necessarily mean that it is the best judgment.
    b) There may be several choices that rank very close together.

       c) The student may want to list criteria that would be of low priority in making a decision about a specific alternative.

       d) The student may want to weigh his/her criteria.

       e) The student may wish to add other criteria to support his/her choice of an alternative. This is pushing for flexibility.

5. Reasons—the teacher encourages the student to support or defend his/her decision by giving reasons for his/her choice.

       a) It is important to allow students to share their ideas and results. There is pleasure in delving into other people's thoughts and ideas and learning goes hand-in-hand with pleasure.

6. Sample warm-ups:

       a) "If you could only eat one kind of food for a whole week, what would you eat? Think of at least five alternatives (choices). While you're thinking about your decisions, consider these criteria:

          1) Do I like it?
          2) Will it be good for me?
          3) Can I afford it?
          4) Will my parents let me?
          5) Will I get tired of it?

          Carefully make your choice. Give reasons for your choice."

       b) "We have read many interesting stories. Which one do you think is the best? Think of three stories that you like. (These are your alternatives.) Consider the following criteria as you make your choice:

          1) Does it have a good ending?
          2) Did it keep me interested?
          3) Would I recommend it to a friend?

E. **Evaluation** is the ability to weigh ideas, looking at the desirability and undesirability of each.

1. It is an attempt to equalize both sides of an idea.
2. The following form may be used.

Figure 2-4
Evaluation Form

Subject

Likes	Dislikes

3. Sample warm-ups:
(When introducing evaluation, push students to strive for the same number of positive and negative points to avoid prejudice.)

a) "Choose a three-syllable word from your list. (Fluency 8.d.). Use the evaluation "T" to list the desirable and undesirable things about the word."

Example:

Octopus	
Desirable	Undesirable

b) "Evaluate the performance of the class yesterday. What was desirable about it? What was undesirable about it?"
c) "Evaluate a book or a character from a story the class has read. What did you find that was good about the story (or character)? What was bad about the book?"

F. **Summary**
1. Each part of each process may be worked on alone, but the teacher should inform children which part is being emphasized.
2. Begin each exercise with a brief oral warm-up.
3. Productive thinking should be the first process to be developed. This could easily take two months the first year.
4. The other processes could be presented in any order.
5. There are blank formats available for some skills, but it is desirable to dress these up to fit the specific assignment.

III. **Creative Problem-Solving** — Creative Problem-Solving is a process developed by Dr. Alex Osborne and Dr. Sidney Parnes that enables individuals to develop their creative skills to help solve problems. The CPS technique encourages development of an open mind, generates the ability to produce quality and original ideas, and promotes greater expression of curiosity.

To ensure a clear understanding of the steps of the CPS process at an elementary school age, it is wise to work on the concept of each step independently and then put all the steps together for the total process.

There are some important factors prerequisite to work on any part of the process. When one is working in the beginning stages, it is important that the situation or activity be one with which the students are not emotionally entangled. The purpose is an understanding of the process, not proof of it.

Basic rules for *brainstorming* or production of ideas underlie every activity at every step:
1. Produce many ideas
2. Hitchhike on other people's ideas
3. Stretch thinking for far-out ideas
4. Defer judgment

Sample Lesson

PROJECT AREA: Creative Problem-Solving (see sample work sheet, Fig. 2-6, page 36).

CURRICULUM AREA: Intermediate — Science — Wildlife Conservation

MATERIALS: Paper, pencil and "Ong, of Canada," a story from *Time to Wonder* (Holt, Rinehart & Winston, 1979), Level 13, 1973.

PRESENTATION:

Teacher Talk

"We know that in the past years, several animals have almost become extinct. Instead of adding to the problem of destruction of wildlife, let's find a way of helping to conserve it. Through the problem-solving process let's solve the following problem situation: How might we help conserve wildlife?"

A. Fact-Finding

"What questions can you ask about wildlife conservation? Use the key words who, what, when, where, and why." Record the questions as the students respond. "To what resources could we go to find answers to each of these questions?" Encourage students to be fluent and flexible in possible resources. Record responses.

B. Problem-Finding

"You need to get to the root of the problem. Restate the problem three times in different ways using the words 'In what ways might we ...' (the IWWMW form). Your first statement might be 'In what ways might we conserve wildlife?' Why do you want to conserve wildlife? Can you make a restatement knowing that? After you have restated the problem at least three times, decide which statement most accurately defines the problem."

C. Idea-Finding

"Using the problem statement you have found, list as many possible solutions as you can. Defer judgment. Don't evaluate, censor, or judge. Anything goes! After you have made your list, circle the best solutions."

D. Solution-Finding

"What standards do you want the solution to meet when you have finished? List four or five criteria. Make a grid like the suggested form in Fig. 2-5, page 36, listing your best ideas down the side and your alternatives across the top. Rate the ideas from one to five for each criteria. Work down, *not* across. Add the total."

Figure 2-5
Solution-Finding Form

CRITERIA

_____

RATE: 5 = excellent
       4
       3
       2
       1 = poor

IDEAS

_____
_____
_____
_____

Figure 2-6
Creative Problem-Solving Work Sheet

NAME _____

Objective:

1. **Fact-Finding.** Determine available facts stated in the problem. Use key words such as WHO, WHAT, WHEN, WHERE and WHY.

    _____
    _____
    _____
    _____

    What other information might you need? Be fluent and flexible in utilizing resources.

    _____
    _____
    _____

2. **Problem-Finding.** Restate the problem at least three ways. Decide which statement most accurately defines the problem.

    1) _____
    _____

    2) _____
    _____

    3) _____
    _____
    _____

3. **Idea-Finding** (Brainstorming, alternatives, etc.). Using the best problem statement, list as many possible solutions as you can. Sketch some pictures. *Defer judgment. Don't evaluate, censor, or judge.* Anything goes! After you have made your list, circle the best ones.

_____

_____

_____

_____

_____

4. **Solution-Finding.** What standards do you want the solution to meet when you have finished? List four or five criteria. Complete work towards solution.

_____

_____

_____

_____

_____

If several answers are possible, make a grid that lists your best ideas down the side and your alternatives across the top (see a Solution-Finding Matrix, page 36). Rate the ideas from one to five for each criteria. Work down, *not* across. Add the total. The highest number will have the best chance for success, according to your criteria.

5. **Acceptance-Finding.** If there is only one possible correct solution, check the solution with the teacher. If several solutions are possible, list reasons why you selected yours.

_____

_____

_____

What steps would you use to implement your solutions?

_____

_____

_____

What problems might you have? How would you prevent those problems? Who might help you?

_____

_____

_____

The following are some hints about the Creative Problem-Solving process:

—Work with the process many times as a group before proceeding individually.

Figure 2-6 (cont'd)

—By limiting each step, it is possible to take a class through the entire process in an hour.

—Many teachers find it very valuable to do the steps as separate activities (taking approximately 20 minutes) several times before running through the entire process.

—Fact-finding is an excellent comprehension tool for use upon completion of a story. It is also a great way to begin a unit. Each person is responsible for finding answers to a certain number of fact-finding questions during the course of the unit.

—Problem-finding is fun to use during a current events class or when studying world problems. (Students try to restate the problem and determine if it is the real problem.)

—Idea-finding can be practiced in one minute or 10 minutes. The teacher or students suggest a topic to brainstorm.

—Solution-finding can be used when making a decision. It can also be fun to use in social studies or language arts. Students weigh the alternatives someone else had in a given situation.

—Acceptance-finding provides students with the opportunity to practice organizing and developing workable plans of action.

3 THE FIRST OF THE 3 R'S: READING

As in other areas of the language arts, many teachers feel that reading instruction is unnecessary for gifted students who are academically talented. Since these students possess word attack, vocabulary, and comprehension skills several years beyond their grade level, teaching reading skills seems a waste of time.

The problem with this thinking lies in defining the term, **reading**. With the emphasis in most classroom reading instruction on the lower-level thinking processes of Bloom's taxonomy, many teachers equate success in reading with the child's ability to pronounce a word, define the word, and use the word in a sentence. The emphasis in instruction is on words!

Reading is not, however, the decoding of words. It is *the creation of visual images*. Think for a moment of a recent novel you have read. If you were asked to recite the first three paragraphs of that novel, it would be an impossible task. Yet you should be able to recall vividly and describe many scenes from the novel. It is the reader's ability to form these visual images from the printed page — the ability to get beneath the words to the images and ideas they represent — that "hooks" one on books.

Unfortunately, in the United States only 17 out of every 100 adults read one or more books a year. Of college graduates, only four out of 10 read one or more books a year.* Certainly many gifted minds are among those who choose not to read. It seems obvious that the less one reads, the less one thinks, for words are the basic tools of thought. Put another way, a simple, nongrowing vocabulary equals a simple, nongrowing mind.

With this in mind, then, the long-range goals of a reading program for gifted students should be 1) to create readers in the full, meaningful sense of the word; and 2) to expand the child's reading, writing, speaking, and **thinking** vocabulary.

Intermediate goals include the following:

1. to help the student toward an awareness and sensitivity to the problems and situations discovered in his or her reading.

2. to spot inconsistencies in the writer's premises, or missing elements in a story.

Bowker Annual of Library and Book Trade Information, 19th ed. (New York: R. R. Bowker Co., 1974).

3. to see new ways to combine objects or ideas and/or discover new uses for information.

4. to solve problems with story characters, to anticipate or forecast events, and to establish criteria for evaluating solutions.

5. to be aware of details that enrich visual images and to appreciate an author's unique style in creation of such images for the reader.

6. to develop an inquiring and ever-expanding mind.

The instructional modules that follow are based on this curriculum model. Topics for these modules were selected because of their particular interest to gifted students. Both primary and intermediate modules are included, suggesting ways to combine independent reading experiences with critical and productive thinking processes.

READING ALOUD TO CHILDREN

While academically talented students usually read well independently, it is essential that the teacher continue to read aloud books so they can be enjoyed and shared together. Especially share books that give children the opportunity to wonder. Children are so easily catapulted into a world of pure academia and, as Albert Einstein said, "The man who no longer wonders, who no longer feels amazement, is as good as dead, a snuffed out candle." Words are the tools of both thought and imagination, and sharing gifted literature with others can lure young genius to the surface. A good piece of literature is not one-way communication. It is a catalyst to facilitate the reader's (or listener's) own source of unfolding thought.

The First Step: READING ALOUD

Select books:
　　To stretch the imagination
　　To extend interests
　　To develop appreciation of fine writing

GOOD BOOKS TO READ ALOUD

Ages Five through Seven

Aardema, Verna. *Who's in Rabbit's House?* (Dial, 1976). *Why Mosquitoes Buzz in People's Ears* (Dial, 1977).

Alexander, Lloyd. *The King's Fountain* (Dutton, 1971). *Coll and His White Pig* (Holt, Rinehart & Winston, 1965). *The Truthful Harp* (Holt, Rinehart and Winston, 1967).

Balet, Jan. *The Fence* (Delacorte, 1969).

Brown, Marcia. *Once a Mouse* (Charles Scribner's Sons, 1961).

Charlip, Remy. *Fortunately* (Parents, 1964).

Crowe, Robert. *Clyde Monster* (Prentice-Hall, 1975).

De Paola, Tomie. *Strega Nona* (Prentice-Hall, 1975).

Haley, Gail. *Noah's Ark* (Atheneum, 1971).

Holl, Adelaide. *The Man Who Had No Dream* (Random, 1969).

Kantrowitz, Mildred. *Maxie* (Parents, 1970).

Kent, Jack. *The Wizard of Wallaby Wallow* (Parents, 1971).

Kraus, Robert. *The Gondolier of Venice* (Windmill, 1976).

Marshall, James. *George and Martha* (Houghton Mifflin, 1972).

Steele, Flora. *Tattercoats* (Bradbury, 1976).

Tresselt, Alvin. *The Dead Tree* (Parents, 1972).

Viorst, Judith. *Alexander and the Terrible, Horrible, No Good, Very Bad Day* (Atheneum, 1972).

Wells, Rosemary. *Noisy Nora* (Dial, 1973).

Williams, Jay. *The Cookie Tree* (Parents, 1967).

Zemach, Harve. *Penny a Look* (Farrar, Straus & Giroux, 1971).

Ages Seven, Eight, and Nine

Alexander, Lloyd. *The Town Cats and Other Tales* (Dutton, 1977). *The Four Donkeys* (Dutton, 1978).

Carmer, Carl. *The Boy Drummer of Vincennes* (Harvey, 1972).

Caudill, Rebecca. *A Certain Small Shepherd* (Holt, Rinehart & Winston, 1965).

Carrick, Donald. *The Foundling* (Dial, 1978).

Cleary, Beverly. *The Mouse and the Motorcycle* (Morrow, 1965).

De Paola, Tomie. *Helga's Dowery* (Prentice-Hall, 1978).

Dahl, Roald. *Charlie and the Chocolate Factory* (Knopf, 1964). *Fantastic Mr. Fox* (Knopf, 1970). *James and the Giant Peach* (Knopf, 1961). *Magic Finger* (Knopf, 1966).

Hunter, Mollie. *A Furlof Fairy Wind* (Harper & Row, 1977).

Kraus, Robert. *Detective of London* (Windmill, 1977).

McGovern, Ann. *Half a Kingdom* (Warne, 1977).

Miles, Miska. *Annie and the Old One* (Little, 1971). *Wharf Rat* (Little, 1972).

Milne, A. A. *World of Pooh* (Dutton, 1957).

White, E. B. *Charlotte's Web* (Harper & Row). *Trumpet of the Swan* (Harper & Row, 1970).

Yolen, Jane. *Girl Who Cried Flowers* (Crowell, 1974). *The Hundredth Dove* (Crowell, 1977). *The Moon Ribbon* (Crowell, 1976). *The Seventh Mandarin* (Seabury, 1970).

Ages Nine, Ten, and Eleven

Armstrong, William. *Sounder* (Harper & Row).

Burch, Robert. *Queenie Peavy* (Viking, 1966).

Byars, Betsy. *The Night Swimmers* (Viking, 1980).

DeJong, Meindert. *Hurry Home Candy* (Harper & Row, 1953).

Konigsberg, Elaine. *The Mixed Up Files* (Atheneum, 1967).

L'Engle, Madeleine. *A Wrinkle in Time* (Farrar, Straus & Giroux, 1962).

Lewis, C. S. *The Lion, the Witch and the Wardrobe* (Macmillan, 1950).

MacKellar, William. *Witch of Glen Gowrie* (Dial, 1978).

Merrill, Jean. *The Pushcart War* (Scott, 1964).

O'Brien, Robert. *Mrs. Frisby and the Rats of Nimh* (Atheneum, 1971).

O'Dell, Scott. *Island of the Blue Dolphins* (Houghton Mifflin, 1960).

Pearce, Philippa. *Tom's Midnight Garden* (Lippincott, 1950).

Sleator, William. *Blackbriar* (Dutton, 1972).

Ages Eleven, Twelve, and Thirteen

Alexander, Lloyd. *The High King* (Holt, Rinehart & Winston, 1968).

Cleaver, Vera, and William. *Where the Lillies Bloom* (Lippincott, 1969).

Cooper, Susan. *The Dark Is Rising* (Atheneum, 1973).

Cunningham, Julia. *Dorp Dead* (Pantheon, 1977).

Engdahl, Sylvia. *Enchantress from the Stars* (Atheneum, 1970).

Forbes, Esther. *Johnny Tremain* (Houghton Mifflin, 1943).

George, Jean. *Julie of the Wolves* (Harper & Row, 1972).

LeGuin, Ursula. *A Wizard of Earthsea* (Parnassus, 1968).

Paterson, Katherine. *Bridge to Terabithia* (Crowell, 1977). *The Great Gilly Hopkins* (Crowell, 1978).

Peck, Richard. *The Ghost Belonged to Me* (Viking, 1975). *Ghosts I Have Been* (Viking, 1977).

Southall, Ivan. *Ash Road* (Reissue, Greenwillow, 1978).

Speare, Elizabeth. *Witch of Blackbird Pond* (Houghton Mifflin, 1958).

Tolkien, J. R. R. *The Hobbit* (Houghton Mifflin, 1938).

Wojciechowska, Maia. *Shadow of a Bull* (Atheneum, 1964).

The Preschool/Primary Reading Experience

Many three-, four- and five-year-olds in gifted preschool/kindergarten programs read fluently. However, the small motor skill development of the children is not usually as advanced as their verbal ability. Therefore, activities in reading with these children must be planned to include a balance of oral responses and manipulative activities.

As demonstrated in this language arts reading module, children at this age are still egocentric and are most interested in topics concerned with self. In addition, books chosen for this module are those that stimulate the developing thinking processes of early childhood—classification, seriation, reversibility, and conservation.

GIFTED LEARNING MODULE NO. 1:
Using the Five Senses

WARM-UP ACTIVITIES
(A pre-school, kindergarten language arts module)

I.   Fluency: The ability to make many responses.
     A.   Name as many things that you enjoy touching as you can.
     B.   List all the sounds you heard on the way to school.
     C.   Name all the things that you have tasted today.

II.   Flexibility: The ability to respond in a variety of areas.
     A.   Name all the sound signals (fire alarm, etc.) that you can.
     B.   List all the things that you would taste at a birthday party.
     C.   Where else can you taste these same things?

III.   Originality: The ability to think and act in new and unique ways.
     A.   What sound signal did you name that no one else named? (Flexibility A).
     B.   Imagine a totally new animal. Use your senses to tell me about him. How would he feel if you touched him? What does he smell like? What does he look like? What sound does he make? If you cooked him and ate him, how would he taste?

IV.   Elaboration: The ability to add to basic ideas.
     A.   Make up a song about one of your senses.
     B.   A bell makes a ringing sound. What other things make ringing sounds?

V.   Planning: The ability to identify the basic elements of a task, the steps and materials necessary to complete the task, and the problems that might be encountered.

    A.   If I wanted to see the sun rise one morning, what would I have to do? (materials, steps, problems).

    B.   How would you go about planning lunch for your friends?

VI.   Forecasting: The ability to link cause and effect.

    A.   Suppose you could not hear. How would your life be different?

    B.   Mother is cooking liver and spinach for dinner. You do not like the way liver and spinach taste. What will happen at dinner time?

VII.   Decision-Making: The ability to examine both positive and negative aspects of any given situation, to establish criteria for making choices, and to select the best alternative in light of established criteria.

    A.   If you had to lose one of your senses, which one would it be? Why?

        Things to think about:

           How much do I use this sense?
           How would it affect my other senses?
           Could I use my other four senses to find out about things?

VIII.   Evaluation: The ability to make choices after examining the good and less desirable aspects of any object or idea.

    A.   Our class is planning a field trip. We want to use all our senses to discover things about this place.

        Decide if the city dump would be a good place to visit.

           List all the good points of going.
           List all the bad points of going.
           Should we go?

IX.   Problem-Solving: The ability to identify all aspects of a problem, examine many possible solutions, and select the best solution.

    A.   You are playing in the woods on a family camping trip. It gets dark much quicker than you expected. It is so dark that you can no longer see to find your way back. What will you do?

           What is the biggest problem?
           Think of as many solutions as you can.
           Which solution will best solve the problem?

EXERCISES

A.   **Feet Feeling**

    1.   Go outside with your teacher.
    2.   Take off your shoes and your socks.
    3.   Now walk around and feel with your feet. Find as many different textures as possible.
    4.   Tell your teacher all the textures that you feel, using as many descriptive words as you can.
    5.   Put a blindfold on. Have a friend lead you around. By feeling with your feet, guess where you are.

B. **The Quiet Evening**
   By Thacher Hurd
   1. Listen to the story *The Quiet Evening*.
   2. Now think of quiet sounds. Name as many as you can.
   3. Which sounds are outdoor sounds? Which sounds are indoor sounds?

   Indoor   **Outdoor**

   _____   _____
   _____   _____
   _____   _____

C. **How Does It Taste**
   You will need: magazines   4 pieces of construction paper
                      scissors   a black crayon
                      paste
   1. Find as many pictures of food as you can.
   2. Paste things that taste salty on the red paper.
      Paste things that taste sour on the blue paper.
      Paste things that taste sweet on the green paper.
      Paste things that taste bitter on the yellow paper.
   3. Use your black crayon to put a letter on each food picture to tell when you would eat it.

      B for breakfast
      L for lunch
      D for dinner
      S for snack

D. **Sing the song** *I Love the Mountains*
   1. Change the word love to a sense word. Decide which word would fit best. Be able to tell why that word fits best.
   2. Use the same melody and make up new words for the song. Keep the same word pattern.
   3. Teach your new song to the class.

E. **Listen to the poem** *The Blind Men and the Elephant*
   1. The blind men are using the sense of touch and then they describe what they feel.
   2. You and three of your friends are going to be the four blind men.
   3. Suggested "elephants"

      a telephone   a (large) pencil sharpener
      a toaster   a lace-up boot
      a mixer   a stuffed animal
      a lamp
   4. Your teacher will blindfold each of you and then place an object in the middle of the four of you. Use a descriptive phrase to say what the object is (if you know) and what it is like.

      Example: "The elephant is like a tree."

F. **What Do I Smell**
    Directions: A teaspoon of the following items is placed on six-inch
    squares of tissue paper: chocolate bits, crushed peppermint pieces,
    orange peelings, strawberry flavored "Kool-aid," butter salt, lemon
    peelings, coffee, dehydrated onion bits (slightly dampened), dried apple
    pieces. The squares are then bundled and tied with string. Two children
    play the game. The first child picks up a bundle at random. He takes a
    sniff and places the bundle in the top circle on the correct square. (If he
    cannot guess, he misses his turn.) Then the second child does the same,
    matching and putting his bundle in the circle at the bottom of the square.
    Three in a row wins!

Smelling Tic-Tac-Toe

G. **What Is the Question?**
    Directions: Draw a picture that shows the question.
    1. The answer is: It feels cold. What is the question?
    _____
    _____

    2. The answer is: It feels rough. What is the question?
    _____
    _____

    3. The answer is: It feels slimy. What is the question?
    _____
    _____

4. The answer is: It feels sticky. What is the question?

_____

_____

5. The answer is: It feels smooth. What is the question?

_____

_____

6. The answer is: It feels soft. What is the question?

_____

_____

7. The answer is: It feels fuzzy. What is the question?

_____

_____

8. The answer is: It feels hot. What is the question?

_____

_____

H. **Do a Senses' Dance**
1. Listen to the music on the tape.
2. Make up a dance that shows how you use your five senses.
3. Show me how you feel about the senses that you are using. For example, if you are showing me the sense of taste and what you are tasting tastes bad, how does your face look?
4. Share your dance with some other people. At the end of your dance have them tell you which sense you were showing first, second, third, fourth, and fifth.

I. **Your Pot of Soup**
1. Listen to the story *Lentil Soup* by Joe Lasker.
2. Make your own favorite kind of soup.
3. Each day add a new ingredient to your soup.
4. Draw your own pot and the ingredients. Number each ingredient so that another person can follow your recipe.

J. **Your Rocket Ship**
1. Suppose your rocket ship has just landed on another planet. Draw a picture of what you see from the window of your spaceship.

K. **The Story** *Arthur's Nose*
1. Listen to the story *Arthur's Nose* by Marc Brown.
2. What if Arthur had decided to change his nose?
3. Make a new ending to the story.

L. *Arthur's Nose*
By Marc Brown

1. Read about Arthur. He has a big nose.

What would be some good things about having a big nose like Arthur's?

What would be some bad things about having a nose like his?

Good Things	Bad Things

2. Arthur is playing a game. Circle the things he could find using only his sense of smell.

loaf of bread	cake
ice cream cone	butterfly
fish	light bulb
pack of gum	fan
jar of applesauce (opened)	lighted fire
record player	cup of coffee
jar of jam (opened)	key
bottle of soda (cap on)	ball

M. **Suppose You Could Not See**

Use your
NOSE
EARS
HANDS

1. Find a friend to play this game with you.
2. Tell your friend what you think it would be like if you could not see.
3. Have your friend tell you what it would be like if he could not see.
4. Go out on the playground. Put on the blindfold. Hold your friend's hand and walk around.
5. Tell your friend all the things that you can hear, smell, and touch.
6. Now let your friend have a turn to wear the blindfold.
7. Tell your teacher a story about the day you could not see.

N. **Look at the story** *Pancakes for Breakfast*
By Tomie De Paola

1. List all the lady's problems. Have your teacher write them down.
2. What was her biggest problem? Have your teacher write it down.
3. Think of as many ways to solve the problem as you can. Have your teacher write them down.
4. Decide on the best solution.
5. Use the tape recorder to tell the whole story, including how you solved her problem.
6. Problems:

7. Biggest Problem:

8. Solutions:

O.   **What Do You See?**
   1.   Look very carefully at the book *Look Again* by Tana Hoban.
   2.   Try to figure out what the picture is before turning the white page.
   3.   Now make your own "looking" book.

   You will need:

   magazines   paper
   scissors   paper with holes
   paste

   4.   Share your book with a friend. See if your friend can tell you what the pictures are.

P.   **Sounds**
   1.   You will need five friends.
   2.   Together, listen to the tape of *The Indoor Noisy Book* by Margaret Wise Brown.
   3.   Decide how you could make a noise for each of the sounds described in the book. You may use things that you find in the classroom, on the playground, or your own voice to make the noise. Bring all of the things back to the listening center.
   4.   Now listen to the tape again. Put the sounds in the right place.
   5.   Share the story, using the sounds you have chosen, with our class.
   6.   Here are pictures of the sounds you will be looking for. They are not in order.

Q.   **How Do You Smell?**
   1.   Remember Muffin, the little dog that had a cold so he had to stay in his room all day? When you have a cold, which one of your senses usually doesn't work very well?

2. Let's suppose Muffin has an ear infection instead of a cold. The doctor puts cotton in his ears so he cannot hear. Muffin has to stay in bed in his room all day. How will he find out what the rest of the family is doing?

He can't hear them.
He can't see them.
He can't touch them.
He can't taste them.

So he must *smell* all the things that the family is doing around the house! Dogs have a very good sense of smell.

3. Tell your teacher all the smells Muffin can smell. They can be indoor and outdoor smells.

R.   A Scavenger Hunt
1. Take five small bags.

Draw an eye on one bag.
Draw an ear on the next bag.
Draw a nose on the next bag.
Draw a hand on the next bag.
Draw a mouth on the next bag.

2. Now take your bags and look for one item to go in each bag.

Put something in your eye bag that you discover with your sense of sight.

Put something in your ear bag that you discover with your sense of hearing.

Put something in your nose bag that you discover with your sense of smell.

Put something in your hand bag that you discover with your sense of touch.

Put something in your mouth bag that you discover with your sense of taste.

3. Show your things to the teacher. Tell her why you think the thing you found fits *best* in the bag that you put it in.

Make a Menu

You will need: magazines
paste
scissors

Cut pictures from magazines that show what you would have for lunch if you could have *anything* you wanted for one week. Paste the pictures on the chart.

SUNDAY	MONDAY
TUESDAY	WEDNESDAY
THURSDAY	FRIDAY
SATURDAY	

S. **I Am Ears**
1. Listen to the story *I Am Eyes — Ni Macho* by Leila Ward.
2. Decide what the pattern of the story is.
3. Make up your own story using the same pattern that you found in *I Am Eyes*.

Your story will be called *I Am Ears*.
4. Have your teacher write your story down for you.
5. Illustrate your story by drawing pictures or cutting out pictures from magazines.
6. Getting started:

After you have decided on the pattern, choose six letters whose sound you know. Think of all the things that you can hear that begin with that letter. Have your teacher write them down.

T. **Plan a Bulletin Board**
Plan and make a bulletin board about your five senses. You may choose one sense or all five of them.

Your teacher will help you use the chart below in your planning.

What?	Materials 1. 2. 3. 4. 5.
Steps 1. 2. 3. 4. 5.	Problems 1. 2. 3. 4. 5.

U.   **It Makes Sense to Buy ...**

Our senses bring us information from the world around us. We like things that are pleasing to our senses. The people who make and sell things know this, so when they make their commercials they try to make us think pleasant thoughts about one (or more) of our senses.

1.   For one week during your regular television-watching times, look carefully at the commercials. Decide which sense (or senses) the commercial is trying hardest to get you to think about.

2.   There is a chart below for you to keep by or on top of your TV set for a week. Each time you see a different commercial, have someone write the name of the thing being advertised. Show the person which column to write it in. Put a check mark (✓) by the commercials that made you really want to have the thing being advertised. Which things would you buy? Circle them.

3.   Think about the commercials that you checked. Think of reasons why they were good. Have someone write the reasons down.

4.   Using the reasons that you thought of, make up a commercial. (See Activity 3.)

5.   Share your commercial with the class.

V. **Be a Designer**

Inventors and designers are people who make new and different things.

There are many people busy inventing and designing things today. After they have made their new products, they want to sell them. In order to sell them, they must advertise.

1. Pretend you are an inventor or designer. You are to design a product that will be pleasing to one or more of our five senses.

Examples:

smell—a perfume designer
sight—a clothes designer
taste—a new breakfast cereal
hearing—a new musical instrument
touch—a cuddly new toy

2. Have your teacher help you with your planning.

What?	Materials 1. 2. 3. 4. 5.
Steps 1. 2. 3. 4. 5. 6. 7.	Problems 1. 2. 3. 4.

3. Make your product.
4. Share your product with your friends.
5. Make a commercial or magazine advertisement about your product.

W. **Young Fluent Thinkers ...**

(Activities with alphabet books)

1. *ABC Bunny* by Wanda Gag (Coward, 1933).
    A wonderful introduction to alliteration ... "L is for Lizard, Look how lazy!"

    How many can children add? D is for dog, digging in the _____.

2. *Ape in a Cape* by Fritz Eichenberg (Harcourt Brace Jovanovich, 1952).
    A study in associations. "Ape in a cape. Goat in a boat."

    Dog on a _____ Cat in a _____ Fox on a _____
    Keep going!

3. *Bruno Munari's ABC* by Bruno Munari (World, 1960).
   Associations with action. From a fly to a feather to a flower to a fish to more flies!

   Select a character. Develop a movement sequence for that character, moving in ABC order from one place or object to another.
4. *A Big City* by Francine Grosbart (Harper & Row, 1966).
   City Country ABC by Marguerite Walters (Doubleday, 1966).
   All around the Town by Phyllis McGinley (Lippincott, 1948).
   Make city and country alphabet books. Find pictures in magazines of things found usually in the city and usually in the country. Make a page for things that begin with each letter of the alphabet. Label the pictures.
5. *Big Golden Animal ABC* by Garth Williams (Golden Press, 1954).
   For the letter *A*, list a very large animal. For *B*, list a very small animal. Alternate large and small with each added letter.
6. *A for the Ark* by Roger Duvoisin (Lothrop, 1952).
   Noah calls the animals to the ark alphabetically. Can you name the animals in alphabetical order?
7. *ABC Alphabet Cookbook* by Dorothy Deers (Schmitt, 1972).
   Here's a toughie! Can you plan a meal from beginning to end, serving foods in alphabetical order?
8. *The B Book* and *C Is for Clown* by Stanley and Janice Berenstain (Random, 1971 and 1972, respectively).
   Write your own story using words that begin with the same letter as many times as possible.
9. *All Butterflies* by Marcia Brown (Charles Scribner's Sons, 1974).
   Paired letters and words are fun to do! All Butterflies, Cats Dance.
10. *Marcel Marceau Alphabet Book* by George Mendoza (Doubleday, 1970).
    Pantomine feelings in ABC order ... let friends guess what the feeling is! Angry, Bashful, Cautious, Daring, Excited ... keep going!
11. *All in a Suitcase* by Samuel Morse (Little, 1966).
    If you are planning a trip, what will you need to take with you? Write your list in ABC order.
12. *Q Is for Duck: An Alphabet Guessing Game* by Mary Elting (Houghton Mifflin, 1980).
    Why is Q for duck? Because ducks quack, of course. What letters can you associate with words?
13. *On Market Street* by Arnold and Anita Lobel (Greenwillow, 1981).
    Study the pictures! Each merchant on Market Street is made up of the wares he sells! The bookseller is made of books, the jeweler of jewels ... construct a modern-day merchant ... use the things he sells to put him together.

X. **Especially for Young Researchers**
1. *A Peaceable Kingdom: A Shaker Abecedarius* by Alice and Martin Provenson (Viking, 1978).
    A book of the life and customs of an earlier people ... in ABC order.
2. *Jambo Means Hello* by Tom and Muriel Feelings (Dial, 1974).
    Swahili words and concepts for each letter of the alphabet.

3. *Ashanti to Zulu: African Traditions.* Illus. by Leo and Diane Dillon, written by Margaret Musgrove (Dial, 1976).
   Customs and ceremonies of 26 tribes of Africa.
4. *Handtalk: An ABC of Finger Spelling and Sign Language* by Remy Charlip (Four Winds, 1974).
5. *Twenty-Six Starlings Will Fly through Your Mind* by Barbara Wersba (Harper & Row, 1980).
   Metaphors, personification, analogies and imagination ... a model to examine, enjoy, and emulate.

Y. **An Exercise in Reversibility**
From Robert Kraus, *The Little Giant* (Harper & Row, 1967).
"I am a giant. I know I am a giant because I have giant whiskers and carry a giant club. But nobody else knows it. Grasshoppers hop at me, bees buzz at me, spiders try to lure me into their webs, and the big giant won't even say HELLO."

I am a _____. I know I am a _____ because I _____
and _____ . But nobody else knows it. _____ ,
_____ , _____ , and the _____.

BIBLIOGRAPHY

Brown, Marc. *Arthur's Nose* (Little, 1976).

Brown, Margaret Wise. *The Indoor Noisy Book* (Harper & Row, 1942).

De Paola, Tomie. *Pancakes for Breakfast* (Harcourt Brace Jovanovich, 1978).

Hoban, Tana. *Look Again* (Macmillan, 1971).

Hurd, Thacher. *The Quiet Evening* (Greenwillow, 1978).

Lasker, Joe. *Lentil Soup* (Whitman, 1977).

Yolen, Jane. Poem "The Blind Men and the Elephants" from "Once a Good Man" in *The Hundredth Dove* (Crowell, 1977).

Ward, Leila. *I Am Eyes—Ni Macho* (Greenwillow, 1978).

GIFTED LEARNING MODULE NO. 2:
Exploring Fairy Tales

An ideal literature area for study in gifted classes is that of folk tales and fairy tales. Young gifted minds *can* be stretched beyond finite limits when they enter the world of imaginative literature for it is a world without boundaries.

It is interesting to note that many of the world's most talented citizens were avid readers of folk tales and fairy tales. Quotations from several of these great minds might well be shared with gifted students.

1. It is imagination that walks hand-in-hand with vision. (Paul Fenimore Cooper).

2. Deeper meaning resides in the tales told me in my childhood than in truth that is taught by life. (Friedrich von Schiller).

3. The present belongs to the sober, the cautious, the routine-prone. But the future belongs to those who do not rein in their imaginations. (Kornei Chukovsky).

The folk tale unit that follows is designed to unleash young imaginations through a blend of content, process, and product.

EXERCISES

I.   Flexible Thinking Activity

   A.   **What's in a Name?**
        1. Read the names of the objects below.

           All the names are taken from fairy tales.
        2. Decide how some of the objects would fit together into different groups.

glass slipper	bread crumbs	shoes	straw
eggs	butter	cake	bed
chair	bowl	crown	golden coach
hooded cloak	horses	lace	apple
coachman	wolf	dwarfs	Grandmother
wicked queen	pancakes	toolshed	rake
hoe	dog	donkey	Bremen
cat	mice	rooster	robbers
forests	castle	fairy	wand

        3. The following are some examples of groups.
           a. Names of foods:
           b. Names of animals:
           c. Names of things to wear:
           d. Names of places:
           e. Names of things that are brown:
        4. See how many more groups you can make.

II.   Flexibility Activity

   A.   **Words, Words, Words!**
        The following words are all taken from fairy tales. *Rearrange the letters* in these scrambled words to make a new word associated with fairy tales. The first letter is the beginning letter for each word.

        kaneblats   b _ _ _ _ _ _ _ _   dogl   g _ _ _ _ _ _ _ _

        tgina   g _ _ _ _ _ _ _ _   tclsae   c _ _ _ _ _ _ _ _

yemno	m_ _ _ _ _ _ _ _	yclru	c_ _ _ _ _ _ _ _
rabe	b_ _ _ _ _ _ _ _	skGlodcoil	G_ _ _ _ _ _ _ _
posu	s_ _ _ _ _ _ _ _	Qneue	Q_ _ _ _ _ _ _ _
pethrsmtoe	s_ _ _ _ _ _ _ _	nosdepio	p_ _ _ _ _ _ _ _
plpae	a_ _ _ _ _ _ _ _	bcmo	c_ _ _ _ _ _ _ _
dWeyn	W_ _ _ _ _ _ _ _	noJh	J_ _ _ _ _ _ _ _
aleMchi	M_ _ _ _ _ _ _ _	zaiL	L_ _ _ _ _ _ _ _
aNna	N_ _ _ _ _ _ _ _	TernkillBe	T_ _ _ _ _ _ _ _
dekito	t_ _ _ _ _ _ _ _	Lnad-rveeN	N_ _ _ _ _ _ _ _
cdoocrlied	c_ _ _ _ _ _ _ _		

III. Evaluation Activity

A. Good, Better, Best!

1. Read the following fairy tales:
   The Three Bears
   Jack and the Beanstalk
   The Tale of Peter Rabbit
2. Form two teams. Try to get students to work for the same number of positive and negative responses.

The Three Fairy Tales Listed Above

| **Desirable** | **Undesirable** |

Which one do you think is the best?
a. Does it have a good ending?
b. Did it keep me interested?
c. Would I want to reread the fairy tale?

3. Take a character from one of the above stories. Evaluate the character. Try for the same number of positive and negative points.

Goldilocks

| **Likes** | **Dislikes** |
| What did you find that was good about the character? | What did you find that was bad about the character? |

IV. Fluency, Seriation Activity

A. Hansel and Gretel

1. Read the fairy tale *Hansel and Gretel.*
2. Find as many compound words as you can in this fairy tale. List them on a piece of paper.
3. Draw five pictures from the story. Be sure to draw them in sequence. Number them one to five.
4. Pretend that you are Hansel and Gretel. Write a story telling what you would have done when you found that you were lost in the woods.

V.   Originality, Vocabulary Building, Communication Activity

A. **Choosing Words for a Story**
1. Paint a picture with words.
2. The following is a description of the scene as Little Black Sambo gets ready to go for a walk into the woods and is met by animals. His mother and father have given him new clothes to wear for his walk into the woods.
3. Choose colorful words to describe this scene. Write the words on this paper.
4. After choosing words to describe this scene, illustrate one of the scenes from this story.

One day Little Black Sambo's mother made him a _____ , _____ , and _____ to wear as he went for a walk into the woods. His father gave him a _____ and _____ to take with him. As Little Black Sambo got into the woods he met _____ . The _____ said, "I am going to eat you." "Please don't eat me," said Little Black Sambo. "I will give you _____." So the _____ took _____ and walked away. Little Black Sambo went farther into the woods. He met a _____ . The _____ was going to kill Little Black Sambo. "Please don't kill me," said Little Black Sambo. "I will give you _____ ." So the _____ took the _____ and walked away. Little Black Sambo walked farther. Soon he met a _____ . "I am going to _____ you," said the _____ . "Please don't," said Little Black Sambo. "I will give you _____ ." So the _____ took _____ from Little Black Sambo and walked away. Little Black Sambo started walking home. He heard a _____ . He became frightened and ran home. When he got home he ate _____ . Then he went _____ .

VI.   Evaluation, Decision-Making Activity

A. **Magic**
Fairy tales make use of magic people, objects, and places.
1. Pretend that these prizes are available. Meet with a group of five classmates.
2. Decide on the first two prizes that your group will choose. All five classmates must be in agreement.
3. You will need to give reasons for your choices.

B. **List of Prizes**
1. A hen that lays a golden egg.
2. A magic wand to take you any place you want to go.
3. A ship that sails on sea and land.
4. Five golden coins that can buy anything.
5. A golden apple that gives you any wish that you make.
6. A dish of candy that always stays filled.
7. A ball that wins every game.

VII.   Communication, Elaboration Activity

A.   **Looking at Style**
Compare these beginnings from *Red Riding Hood.* Tell which one is an adaptation and which one was written by the original author.

> Once there was a sweet little maid who lived with her father and mother in a pretty little cottage at the edge of the village. At the further end of the wood was another pretty cottage and in it lived her grandmother.

> Once there was a pretty little girl who lived with her brothers, sisters, mother, and father in a large house in the middle of the town. At the far end of the town was another pretty house and in it lived her aunt.

Try adding new and colorful words to the story beginning below. Use nouns.

> Once there was a wolf, and the wolf frightened _____. He frightened _____ , the _____ , the _____ , and the _____ . He frightened all the _____ and the _____ in the _____ except one. (Can you continue with the story?)

VIII.   Synthesis Activity

A.   **The Three Bears**
1.   Read the fairy tale *The Three Bears.*
2.   Think where Goldilocks was when the three bears came home.
3.   Think what Goldilocks was doing when the three bears came home.
4.   SUPPOSE:

Suppose that some robbers had arrived at the cottage of the three bears where Goldilocks was before the three bears had arrived home.

5.   Think about these questions.
a.   What might have happened to Goldilocks?
b.   What might have happened to the three bears?
c.   What might have happened to the robbers?
6.   Write your answers on your own paper.
7.   If you wish, you may illustrate one or more of the scenes showing what might have happened to the characters listed above.

B.   **What If?**
1.   Choose any fairy tale listed below.
> *Hansel and Gretel*
> *Rumpelstiltskin*
> *Snow White*
> *Red Riding Hood*
2.   Read it.

3. Write a different ending for the fairy tale.
4. Do as many as you wish.
5. *Hansel and Gretel*:
   a. What if the witch had not died?
   b. What would have happened to Hansel and Gretel?
6. *Rumpelstiltskin*:
   a. What if the queen had not thought of his name?
   b. What would have happened to the queen?
   c. What would Rumpelstiltskin have done with the baby?
7. *Snow White*:
   a. What if Snow White had not come back to life?
8. *Red Riding Hood*:
   a. What if Red Riding Hood's father had not heard her scream and had not come along in time to kill the wolf?

IX.　　Forecasting Activity

A. **Rumpelstiltskin**
   1. Read the fairy tale *Rumpelstiltskin*.
   2. Predict the lives of some of the characters after the story ends.
   3. Use the following for examples:
      a. For example: At the end of the fairy tale, Rumpelstiltskin sank into the ground. Predict how he will live in the ground.
      b. For example: The miller's daughter who became the queen was able to keep her baby because she guessed Rumpelstiltskin's name. Predict what she and her baby will do after the story ends.
   4. Write your predictions on paper. You may also illustrate them if you wish.

X.　　Flexibility, Forecasting, Synthesis Activity

A. **Sleeping Beauty**
   1. Read the fairy tale *Sleeping Beauty*.
   2. Think of the situations below. Predict changes that might happen.
      a. What would have happened if only the curse had fallen upon the princess to sleep for 100 years and not upon anyone else or anything else in the kingdom?
      b. What changes would the princess find when she awoke after the 100 years if she had been the only one who had fallen asleep?
      c. Write your predictions in the form of a story or illustrate them in a picture.

XI.　Planning, Problem-solving Activity

　　A.　**Puss in Boots**
　　　　1.　Read the fairy tale *Puss in Boots.*
　　　　2.　Read the story below that has been made up about Puss in Boots. Then read the information under "Suppose." Decide how Puss in Boots could be rescued.

　　　　　　　One summer afternoon, an enchantress left Puss in Boots on a roof too high to jump off.

　　　　3.　Suppose: The building where Puss in Boots was on the roof was surrounded by quicksand.

　　　　　　Suppose: The miller's two elder sons stood guard on the outside of the quicksand.

　　B.　**How Would You Rescue Puss in Boots?**
　　　　What are the basic problems to overcome?
　　　　1.　_____
　　　　2.　_____
　　　　3.　_____
　　　　What can you do to solve each problem?
　　　　1.　_____
　　　　2.　_____
　　　　3.　_____
　　　　Make a list of all materials and equipment you would need to accomplish the rescue. Give the use of each.

XII.　Curiosity, Elaboration Activity

　　A.　**The Musicians of Bremen**
　　　　1.　Use a tape of the fairy tale *The Musicians of Bremen.*
　　　　2.　Listen to the story. Just close your eyes and think about it.
　　　　3.　Then listen to the story a second time. Use the book to look at the pictures.
　　　　4.　Close your eyes. Imagine what it would be like to be one of the animals in the story journeying on the road to the town of Bremen.
　　　　5.　Think of things that would be seen, things that might happen to you, and whom you might meet on the way.
　　　　6.　Put your ideas on paper. Use either crayons or colored chalk.

XIII.　Analysis Activity

　　A.　**What Is the Question?**
　　　　Think about the fairy tales. Read the answer. It is about a fairy tale. Write a question that would fit the answer.
　　　　1.　The answer is A CANDY HOUSE. What is the question?
　　　　　　_____

　　　　2.　The answer is GLASS SLIPPER. What is the question?
　　　　　　_____

3. The answer is A POISONED APPLE. What is the question?

_____

4. The answer is PANCAKE. What is the question?

_____

5. The answer is CABBAGES. What is the question?

_____

6. The answer is PUSS IN BOOTS. What is the question?

_____

XIV. Flexibility, Originality, Elaboration, Communication Activity

A. **The Other Side of the Story**
Writers of fairy tales present "good" characters as though they can do no wrong. It is acceptable for a good character to trick a bad character but wrong for a bad character to trick a good one.
1. Read the fairy tale *Jack and the Beanstalk.*
2. Here is a possible other side of the story as told by the giant in the fairy tale *Jack and the Beanstalk.*
3. Read this other side of the story.

"From my youth I worked very hard and became wealthy enough to live in a huge castle in a beautiful country. Because I checked some of my possessions each evening to see that nothing had been stolen, some people thought I was greedy. I was not greedy but only wanted to make sure that some lazy person was not taking advantage of my hard work."

"After missing two bags of gold and my little brown hen, I had to be very watchful. When my golden harp called out, 'Master, Master,' I had to follow the thief to protect my possessions. I was killed because I was doing what the head of every household would do."

4. Read another fairy tale.
5. Select a fairy tale villain to transform into a hero or heroine by telling his/her side of the story.

XV. Analysis, Evaluation, Forecasting, Communication Activity

A. **Tic-Tac-Toe Using Fairy Tales**
Complete any three squares down, across, or diagonally. If you need help, read some of the fairy tales. Think about the characters from fairy tales.

The Poor Miller's Son	Was made a wealthy man by his cat.	His soup had been eaten and his chair had been broken.	Changed Cinderella into a Princess.	Teeny Tiny Bear
Fairy Godmother				
Red Riding Hood	Was always in trouble because of his size.	Was almost eaten by a wolf.	Left a poisoned comb in Snow White's hair.	Tom Thumb
				Wicked Queen
Dick Whittington	The church bells encouraged him to go to London.	A fairy who used magic.	Was killed because he was greedy.	
The Giant				Tinker Bell

XVI. Reversibility, Flexible Thinking, Elaboration, Evaluation Activity

A. **Snow White and the Seven Dwarfs**
   1. Read this part of *Snow White and the Seven Dwarfs*.

      Snow White's cruel stepmother was a wicked queen. The wicked queen was jealous because the magic mirror told her the truth that Snow White was more beautiful than she was. Because she was jealous she made many attempts to end Snow White's life.
   2. Rewrite this story from a different point of view.

      Suggestion: Snow White's stepmother was happy because the one person who was more beautiful than she was her stepdaughter, Snow White.
   3. Use this different point of view.
   4. Write how this happiness reflected in the way she would have treated Snow White in contrast to the way she treated her in the original story.

XVII. Planning, Problem-solving Activity

A. **Snow White**
   1. Read the fairy tale *Snow White and the Seven Dwarfs*.
   2. Read this revised account of the tale.
   3. Read the information listed under "Suppose."
   4. Decide how Snow White could be rescued.

      When Snow White was 10 years old she was locked in a cottage in the woods by the wicked queen who lived at the edge of the woods. The cottage was surrounded by tall trees with no roads leading to the cottage.
   5. Suppose: The woods were filled with deadly snakes and vicious wild animals.

      Suppose: No one would try to rescue Snow White because of the jealous queen. What would happen to Snow White?

B. **How Would You Rescue Snow White?**
What are the basic problems to overcome?
1. _____
2. _____
3. _____

What can you do to solve each problem?
1. _____
2. _____
3. _____

Make a list of all materials or equipment you would need to accomplish the rescue of Snow White.

Tell the use of each.

Use paper from the activity table.

XVIII. Originality Activity
A. **Epitaph**
1. Read three fairy tales.
2. Write epitaphs for three fairy tale characters. The lines should tell something about the characters or the character's life.
3. The following are three examples.
   a. Character: Giant
      from the fairy tale *Jack and the Beanstalk.*
      Epitaph: H is
                G reed
                W as
                H is
                E nd
   b. Character: Stepmother
      from the fairy tale *Snow White and the Seven Dwarfs.*
      Epitaph: J ealousy
                R uled
                H er
                L ife
   c. Character: Dwarf
      from the fairy tale *Snow White and Rose Red.*
      Epitaph: W as
                M ean
                A nd
                U ngrateful
4. Write epitaphs for three characters from fairy tales.

XIX. Analysis, Communication, Decision-making Activity

A. **Telegrams**
The following characters from fairy tales wish to send a message. They want the message to be a telegram. Each character has enough money to pay for 25 words. Shorten each message to 25 words. The names of the sender and the receiver are free.

To: Grandmother

While walking to your house this morning, I met a wolf. Not knowing what a wicked beast he was, I told him where I was going. He arrived at your house before I did, put on your cap, crept under your bedclothes. I did not recognize him and began talking with him. My father saved me by cutting off his head. You may expect me to visit you tomorrow.

Little Red Riding Hood

TELEGRAM:

To: The man who gave me the bean

Your beans made a stalk that reached the sky. At the top of the stalk was a castle inhabited by a wealthy giant. I climbed the stalk three times. The first time I took two bags of gold from the giant and ran home with them. The second time I took a little hen that laid golden eggs. The third time I took the giant's golden harp. This time the giant came after me, so I cut the stalk. The giant fell and was killed. Hope you can let me know what happened to my cow.

Jack

TELEGRAM:

To: My stepmother and stepsisters

My fairy godmother prepared me for the two balls. She changed a pumpkin into a coach, six mice into six horses, a rat into a coachman, and six lizards into six footmen. She made me a lovely princess by tapping me on the shoulder. Each evening at twelve o'clock, I was changed into a ragged girl. On the second evening I danced so long that I had to hurry away and lost my glass slipper. Luckily, it did not fit anyone else. I wish you could realize how happy I am since I married the prince.

Cinderella

TELEGRAM:

XX.   Fluency, Flexibility, Originality, Elaboration,
Decision-making Activity

A. **Role-Playing**
1. Read the fairy tale *The Sleeping Beauty.*
2. Read again the part that is printed below. It is taken from the fairy tale *The Sleeping Beauty.*
3. "After the Princess had opened her eyes, she and the Prince went downstairs. The whole court awoke. Everything in the castle began to stir and pick up where it had left off one hundred years ago."
4. Have class members choose some of the scenes listed below to role-play.
   a. Have class members represent the prince, the princess, the king, the queen, the cook, the kitchen maid, the horse, and the dogs. Each class member should take up the activities of the person whose role he/she is playing on the day when the kingdom awoke from 100 years of sleep.
   b. Have class members play the parts of the king and queen and the prince and princess on the wedding day.
   c. Have class members play the parts of the cook and the kitchen maid as they plan the wedding banquet.
   d. Have members of the class play the parts of people who lived outside of the castle. They should give their reactions to the awakening of the castle.

XXI.   Originality, Planning, Vocabulary Activity

A. **Writing a Play**
1. Read the fairy tale *The Elves and the Shoemaker.*
2. Change the story into a play.
3. Decide the number of acts needed for the play.
4. Decide the number of scenes needed for each act.
5. Use the characters listed below.

shoemaker	customer in the shoe shop
shoemaker's wife	two elves

6. Write the play. Remember the form to be used for a play. Example:
    Shoemaker: I work so hard. I try to be honest. The harder I work, the poorer I become.
7. Continue the play using the beginning from number six.

B. **The Golden Goose**
1. Read the fairy tale *The Golden Goose.*
2. Choose a partner.
3. Be able to dramatize the scene from the story *The Golden Goose* when Simpleton meets the little gray-haired man and shares his lunch with him.

4. Example:

    Gray-haired man: May I have one bite of your cake and a sip of your wine?

    Simpleton: It's only a cinder cake. And this is no wine, only sour beer.
5. Continue the conversation between the two characters.
6. When you have it ready, sign a card telling the date and time that you would like to present it to the class.
7. It would be interesting to have your dramatization tape-recorded. Other boys and girls might enjoy listening to the conversation part after they have read the fairy tale *The Golden Goose.*

BIBLIOGRAPHY

Titles suggested are only a few of the many excellent versions of traditional tales.

Andersen, Hans Christian. *Anderson's Fairy Tales* (Collins, 1975).

Arbuthnot, May Hill. *Arbuthnot Anthology of Children's Literature* (Scott, 1961).

Bannerman, Helen. *Little Black Sambo* (Lippincott, 1923).

De Regniers, Beatrice. *Red Riding Hood* (Atheneum, 1972).

Galdone, Paul. *The Three Bears* (Seabury, 1972).

Grimm Brothers. *Grimms' Fairy Tales* (Charles Scribner's Sons, 1960). *Elves and the Shoemaker* (Charles Scribner's Sons, 1960). *The Golden Goose* (Charles Scribner's Sons, 1961). *Hansel and Gretel* (Delacorte, 1971). *Musicians of Bremen* (Harcourt Brace Jovanovich, 1955). *Rumplestiltskin* (Walck, 1970). *Snow White* (Farrar, Straus, & Giroux, 1972).

Perrault, Charles. *Sleeping Beauty* (Crowell, 1977).

GIFTED LEARNING MODULE NO. 3:
Reading Junior Novels

Successful programs for the gifted include as many student choices of materials and activities as possible. One ideal area for providing a free choice of materials is in the sharing of junior novels in middle- to upper-elementary gifted classes.

In this module, children form their own review committees or discussion groups and determine within each group what the final products of the literature study will be.

Each review group is charged with developing a unique product to share their literature with others. Groups are *not* confined to using resources found only within the classroom or the school.

One problem that may arise concerns the kinds of questions discussed in the group. Since many of these children have had excessive exposure to *content* questions, they may need several brainstorming sessions dealing with divergent questions.

For a successful brainstorming session, introduce the following types of questions. They can be applied to a familiar tale, with students developing similar questions, or an unfamiliar tale can be shared. The questions included here are from a tale that gifted students of *all* ages seem to enjoy. Following the question model are examples of activities based on junior novels designed to foster higher-level thinking skills.

Divergent Questioning Model: ("Once a Good Man" from *The Hundredth Dove* by Jane Yolen).

Quantity Question: How many ways might have the man and the angel traveled through the sky?

Reorganization Question: What would have happened if the angel had refused the man's request?

Supposition Question: Suppose that heaven in the story HAD been filled with clouds, choirs, robes, and rainbows. How would this have changed the meaning of the story?

Viewpoint Question: How would the good man's cottage have looked to a king?

Involvement Question: If you found an angel on your doorstep, what would you say or do?

Forced Association Question: How are the stories *Once a Good Man* and O'Henry's *Gift of the Magi* alike?

Analysis: When were you first aware of the reason the people in heaven looked well fed?

Syntheses: Read several other parables. How would you define a parable? Using your definition, write an original parable.

Evaluation: Read several other short stories by Jane Yolen and by another author. Which author do you most enjoy reading? Give reasons for your choice.

EXERCISES

I.   Fluency Activity   *King of the Wind*
                                     by Marguerite Henry
                                     1949 Newbery Medal Winner

A. Another Handout
Agba was a deaf mute. As a result, his hands became more important to him. Make a list of the things a hand usually does. The think about Agba and continue to enumerate as many other hand activities as possible. The list has been started for you. When you finish all you can, score yourself with the table given below.

1. wave	8. _____	14. _____	20. _____
2. write	9. _____	15. _____	21. _____
3. tickle	10. _____	16. _____	22. _____
4. _____	11. _____	17. _____	23. _____
5. _____	12. _____	18. _____	24. _____
6. _____	13. _____	19. _____	25. _____
7. _____			Continue

Score Yourself
15 . . . You found just a handful!
25 . . . You've got a handle on this idea!
40 . . . You've done a handsome job!

II.   Planning Activity   *Call It Courage*
                                     by Armstrong Sperry
                                     1941 Newbery Medal Winner

A. Resourceful Mafatu
Pretend you are Mafatu. You must survive on a strange and primitive island. This takes courage. List one object that begins with each letter in the word "courage" that you would take along to survive. An adjective with a noun is permitted. For example, *C* could be "canoe" (a noun alone) or *C* could be "coconut shell" (an adjective and a noun).

Good luck and be brave!

C_____

O_____

U_____

R_____

A_____

G_____

E_____

III.   Vocabulary Extension Activity   *The Door in the Wall*
       by Marguerite De Angeli
       1950 Newbery Medal Winner

A. **Language**

Medieval to Modern and Back Again

In the book *The Door in the Wall,* many words appeared that seemed strange but that are in common use in today's language. Can you match the medieval form of the word with its present-day word? You may need to use the dictionary. Place the correct letter on the line in front of the number to match yesteryear's word with today's.

Yesteryear's Word

_____ 1. wind hole
_____ 2. bannock
_____ 3. hoodman-blind
_____ 4. quill
_____ 5. bedchamber
_____ 6. minstrel
_____ 7. hosen
_____ 8. guild
_____ 9. hospice
_____ 10. pickaback

Today's Word

a. bedroom
b. pen
c. pair of stockings
d. window
e. labor union
f. blindman's bluff
g. piggy-back
h. inn
i. musician or entertainer
j. corn bread

B. **Homophones**

Following are five present-day words. These words are homophones. This means that there is another word for each of these, and it is pronounced exactly the same but has a different meaning. Give the homophone for each. They are words found in the book.

1. night _____
2. fryer_____
3. fare _____
4. male_____
5. gate _____

IV.   Elaboration Activity   *The Door in the Wall*
                                       by Marguerite De Angeli
                                       1950 Newbery Medal Winner

A. **Surname Search**
    During the Middle Ages, there were often several men in a single
    town all known simply as "John." This was, indeed, a confusing
    problem. Men had only first names! To clear up the confusion,
    surnames (last names) were added. Surnames generally came from a
    person's occupation, a physical characteristic or ability one had, a
    place where one lived, a person's father's name, or a person's
    mother's name.

    What surnames could be given to these Middle Age lads?
    1.   Your name is JOHN. What might your surname be if your
         father makes armor for the king's knights? _____.
    2.   Your name is LUKE. What might your surname be if your
         father rings the bells in the village to warn others of danger?
         _____.
    3.   Your name is JOSIAH. What might your surname be if your
         father tends the sheep for the lord of the castle?
         _____.
    4.   Your name is MARTIN. What might your surname be if your
         father is the cook for the lord of the castle? _____.
    5.   Your name is MARK. What might your surname be if your
         family lives at a ford and helps people cross the stream?
         _____.
    6.   Your name is SYLVESTER. What might your surname be if
         your father works in the castle doing odd jobs because he is
         lame? _____.
    7.   Your name is DAVID. Your father's name is John. What
         might your surname be? _____.
    8.   Your name is GEOFFREY. You live with your father and
         mother and your father watches over the forests and parks of
         the lord of the castle. What might your surname be?
         _____.
    9.   Your name is ANDREW. Your father works for the lord of
         the castle and everyone knows him because he has very white
         hair and a white beard. What might your surname be?
         _____.
    10. Your name is PETER. Your father is dead and your mother
         works at the castle for the queen doing weaving. What might
         your surname be? _____.

V.   Classification Activity   *From the Mixed-up Files of Mrs. Basil E. Frankweiler*
by E. L. Konigsburg
1968 Newbery Medal Winner

A. **Museum Muddle**
The curator of the Metropolitan Museum of Art has asked Jamie and Claudia for their assistance. After having some art works on special display in the Great Hall on the main floor, they now need to be returned to their proper rooms.

"After hiding out in there for a week, that's easy!" exlaimed Jamie.

"Hiding *out in*? What kind of language is that?" snapped Claudia.

"American James Kincaidian language. Aw, baloney! Let's get started."

Your job is to help Jamie and Claudia tell the museum staff in which room to return each piece of art. Place the correct letter of the room in front of the name of the art work. (Note: You may need to use reference books and/or art reference books found in the 700s.)

A.   Egyptian Room
B.   American Wing
C.   Medieval Art
D.   Far Eastern Art
E.   European Paintings and Sculpture
      (Dutch, English, French, Italian, Spanish, fifteenth to nineteenth Century)

_____ 1.   "Don Manuel" by Francisco Goya
_____ 2.   "Midnight Ride of Paul Revere" by Grant Wood
_____ 3.   "Figure of a Horse," white jade. Ch'ing dynasty, 1662-1722
_____ 4.   Armored knight
_____ 5.   "Washington Crossing the Delaware" by Emanuel Leutze
_____ 6.   Painted Porcelain Teapot, China, 1936-1975
_____ 7.   "The Nativity" by Fra Angelico
_____ 8.   Painted Ceiling Patterns from Tomb of 2 Sculptors, Thebes, 1400 B.C.
_____ 9.   "The Card Players" by Paul Cezanne
_____10.   Queen Hatshepsut in Limestone, eighteenth dynasty
_____11.   "In the Boat" by Edouard Manet
_____12.   Wool Bedcover, Connecticut River Valley, 1796

VI.   Research Skills Activity

A. **Meeting a Master**
Answer the questions below to fill in the blanks and get a portrait of a great Renaissance master, Michelangelo.

```
 1.              M _ _ _ _ _
 2.              _ _ _ I _
 3.    _ _ _ _ _ _ _ C _ _ _ _
 4.          _ _ _ H _ _ _ _
 5.            _ _ E _ _
 6.          _ L _ _ _ _ _ _
 7.          _ A _ _ _ _ _
 8.      _ _ _ _ N _ _
 9.        _ _ G _ _ - _ _ _ _
10.          _ _ E _ _ _ _ _
11.          _ _ L _ _ _
12.    _ _ _ _ _ _ O _ _
```

B. **Questions**

1. Which influential and prominent Italian family helped Michelangelo a great deal?

2. Which work of Michelangelo's was carved from flawed marble and unveiled in 1504?

3. Where did Michelangelo paint his scenes of "The Creation" and "Last Judgment"?

4. Besides being an artist and a sculptor, what other type artist was Michelangelo?

5. Which sculpture did Michelangelo do several of, the most famous of which is in Rome?

6. In which Italian city besides Rome did Michelangelo work and study?

7. In which Italian town was Michelangelo born?

8. Michelangelo knew the famous artist who painted the "Mona Lisa." Who was he?

9. How old was Michelangelo when he died?

10. What are paintings done on wet plaster called?

11. Which pope commissioned Michelangelo to paint "The Creation" and "Last Judgment"?

12. What was Michelangelo's surname?

VII. Vocabulary Extension Activity

Mrs. Firsby and the Rats of Nimh
by Robert C. O'Brien
1972 Newbery Medal Winner

A. **Down the Rat Hole**

Explain the meaning of these sentences with "rat" or "rats" in them.

1. Oh, rats!_____

2. He's a pack rat._____

3. Even rats desert a sinking ship._____

4. He's going to rat on me._____

5. This shirt is getting ratty looking.____

6. Welcome to the rat race._____

7.   You can't find anything in that rat's nest!_____
8.   Do you rat your hair?_____

Use *Bartlett's Familiar Quotations* from the reference section and tell where these quotations about rats come from and who the author is.

"I begin to smell a rat." _____ by _____.

Rats.
They fought the dogs and killed the cats,
And bit the babies in the cradles,
And ate the cheeses out of the vats,
And licked the soup from the cooks' own ladles."
_____ by _____

VIII.   Classification, Originality Activity

A.   **An Adventure with Acronyms**
        Acronyms are a way of life in our society. In the book *Mrs. Frisby and the Rats of Nimh*, the acronym NIMH was very, very important. NIMH stands for the National Institute of Mental Health.
        Since this story was a sort of make-believe tale, what else could the acronym NIMH stand for?_____
        Suppose the other animals in this story belonged to some special group or organization. Tell what you think the letters might stand for in these acronyms.
1.   Jeremy belongs to a bird union C.A.W. _____
2.   Dragon belongs to C.A.T.C.H. _____
3.   The owl and Mr. Ages belong to a select society called W.I.S.E. _____
4.   Brutus and Justin belong to a special committee called G.U.A.R.D. _____
5.   Rats not from NIMH belong to S.T.E.A.L._____

IX.   Planning, Problem-solving Activity

A.   **Her Heart's Desire**
        Two junior novels you won't want to miss are:
        Misty and Me
        by Barbara Girion
            and
        Turkey Legs Thompson
        by Jean McCord

        Kim's mother announces to the family that she has taken a full-time job. This in itself would not be so terrible except for the fact that the long-promised dog on which Kim had her heart set will not be coming. And then the idea strikes! Why not adopt a puppy from the local dog pound and hire a puppy sitter to look after it until things calm down at home. What began as a great idea soon becomes a financial drain as Kim discovers that in addition to paying a dog sitter $6.00 a week, there are also bills for food, a dog license, immunizations, and a number of other things. She receives an allowance of $3.00 per week. How can she afford to keep the long-desired pet? (from *Misty and Me*).

No one really seemed to care about Turkey Legs (Betty Ann) Thompson, except when she didn't do all of the things she was supposed to do. This included looking after her little brother and sister, going to school, staying out of fights, not forging her mother's signature on absence slips, telling the truth, and being generally responsible. Betty Ann's mother and father are divorced and, while mom earns the living, most of the responsibility for the family falls on Betty Ann's shoulders. Her dream of the bicycle that would open up a whole new world of freedom for her seems far away. No matter how long she saves, at 25 cents a week it would take 20 years to get the bike ... unless ... (from *Turkey Legs Thompson*).

Is there any way Kim and Turkey Legs can acquire the money needed so that each girl can achieve her heart's desire?

X.   Decision-making Activity

A.   **Consequences ! ! !**
       You are a young girl living in an ancient world 2,000 years ago. You are very good at both inventing and discovering things. Many of your inventions have helped those around you by making their work easier.
       Your cleverness becomes known to the ruler of the land, and you are given all that you need to invent even more things for the enjoyment and the good of all people.
       One invention that you stumble upon quite by accident is a powder that will explode and propel objects with great force. Realizing the harm that this powder can do, you are determined to tell no one of this discovery. However, the head of the king's warriors uncovers your secret and tells the king.
       When you refuse to reveal the source of the ingredients of this black powder, you are thrown into the dungeon where you will remain until you do the king's bidding.

Examine the consequences

**If You Continue to Refuse
to Tell the Secret**   **If You Tell the Secret**

_____   _____
_____   _____

Are there other alternatives?

_____   _____
_____   _____

To discover how one young girl solved this problem read: *Clever-Lazy: The Girl Who Invented Herself* by Joan Bodger.

B. **Changes! Changes! Changes!**

Inventions DO change our lives! Sometimes these changes are small or sometimes quite drastic.

Both the electric light and television have made major changes in the way people live today compared with life 100 years ago.

Can you envision life 100 years from now? You may be able to if you can project the changes that will come about as a result of technology available today. What changes in life style would you predict as a result of:

1. **Solar Power**   **Home Computers**   **Your Choice**

2. The science of cold is just coming of age. Some humans have had their bodies frozen after death in the hope that a cure for their disease will be found and applied when the body is thawed. What problems can you project if this becomes possible?_____

XI.   Problem-solving Activity

A. **The Spy!**

You are the youngest member of a "me-generation" family. Your mother, your dad, and your two older sisters are so busy with their own lives that they rarely pay attention to you, except to comment now and then on your "lively imagination." Much of your time is spent in a secret retreat near your house, observing the actions of others but unseen by them. And then it happens!

You are an eyewitness to the murder of your elderly neighbor (with whom you have never managed to get along). You see all the details of the crime EXCEPT the murderer's face. No one, however, will listen to you or believe your story. Suddenly you are involved in a series of unexplained accidents. Has someone been listening after all? The murderer? What will you do now?

1. State the major problem in two different ways._____

2. List any problems that contribute to the major problem._____

3. List as many possible solutions to the problem as you can in the solution box. Make another box if you need more space.

4. In the space provided, list the probable consequences of each solution.

Possible Solution(s)   Consequences

5. Decide on one best solution. Tell why you chose the solution over all the others._____

_____

6. Read: *The View from the Cherry Tree* by Willo Davis Roberts.

XII. Forecasting Activity

A. **The Fortuneteller**
   You are 11 years old, the middle girl in a large farm family. Your days are spent cropping corn and bugging potatoes; yet you are sure the future must hold much more for you than these mundane chores. You manage to save enough money (a whole 25 cents) to pay the town fortuneteller to tell you that some day you will be rich and that the potato fields will be left far behind; instead, in a deep and somber voice, the fortuneteller says:_____

_____

   Is there anything you will do now as a result of the fortune that you have never done before?_____

_____

   In the book, *Naomi*, by Berniece Rabe, Naomi DOES go to a fortuneteller and does not hear what she expects to hear. While Naomi's good sense tells her that NO ONE can predict the future, still ... it was such an awful fortune, she can't help brooding about it and changing her ways to cope with it.

XIII. Evaluation Activity

A. Read: *Tuck Everlasting* by Natalie Babbitt
   You are wandering in the woods alone. It is a warm day and you stop beside a cool spring to take a drink. Just as your lips are about to touch the water, you are stopped from drinking by a young boy. He explains that the spring contains the power of youth. Those who drink from it will have life everlasting. He suggests that you wait a few years and then drink the water. When you reach the age of 17 life everlasting will seem like a great idea. Or will it?
   Make a decision: Should those who discover the spring drink from it?

Reasons to Drink   Reasons Not to Drink
_____
_____
_____

   Something to think about. If you had one bottle of the magic water and decided not to drink it, what would you do with it? Why? Teachers' Note: In any evaluation activity the student must list as many pros as cons!

BIBLIOGRAPHY

Babbitt, Natalie. *Tuck Everlasting* (Farrar, Straus & Giroux, 1975).

Bodger, Joan. *Clever-Lazy: The Girl Who Invented Herself* (Atheneum, 1979).

De Angeli, Marguerite. *Door in the Wall* (Doubleday, 1950).

Girion, Barbara. *Misty and Me* (Charles Scribner's Sons, 1979).

Henry, Marguerite. *King of the Wind* (Rand, 1948).

Konigsburg, Elaine. *From the Mixed-up Files of Mrs. Basil E. Frankweiler* (Atheneum, 1967).

McCord, Jean. *Turkey Legs Thompson* (Atheneum, 1979).

O'Brien, Robert C. *Mrs. Frisby and the Rats of NIMH* (Atheneum, 1971).

Rabe, Berniece. *Naomi* (Nelson, 1975).

Roberts, Willo Davis. *View from the Cherry Tree* (Atheneum, 1975).

Sperry, Armstrong. *Call It Courage* (Macmillan, 1940).

Yolen, Jane. *The Hundredth Dove & Other Tales* (Crowell, 1977).

4 THE SECOND R: WRITING

Many teachers would agree that writing skills of children are commensurate with their reading abilities. Thus, our concern in development of writing expertise among the academically talented lies not in simply improving grammar, spelling, sentence and paragraph construction, but in helping children to develop their ideas and to communicate them to others.

It is true that students in general are required to do much less writing than students of earlier years. The writing tasks most emphasized in schools today require filling in blanks, or reports done as work sheets, with little opportunity provided for composition. Teachers' comments on student papers most often center on accuracy of content or correctness of mechanics of writing rather than concern with ideas and the way in which those ideas are expressed. The teacher of gifted students must realize that, just as in reading, we must in writing get the mechanics out of the way to get to the ideas underneath.

James Moffett reaches the heart of the matter in another way. He says:

Far too long and far too much, we have thought of reading and writing as technical language matters when the fact is that composing and comprehending are deep operations of mind and spirit.*

Our concern in working with gifted children in writing is, once again, with teaching them to think critically and productively. Children who have experienced numerous prewriting activities in brainstorming, fluent and flexible thinking, planning, forecasting, decision-making, communication, and problem-solving will transpose these newly acquired skills to their written work.

THE WRITING PROCESS

Observations of young children show that writing is first a process of mentally visualizing (and often physically illustrating) a scene or idea. Young children will draw a scene first and then label it. They do not create a picture to fit a label. Yet we often attempt to give children labels in the form of story titles or topics and expect them to write on demand.

---

*Moffett, James. *A Student-Centered Language Arts Curriculum, Grades K-13* (Houghton Mifflin, 1968), p. 23.

Obviously, a house cannot be built without tools. The mechanics of writing must be taught, but only after the creative process is complete. Children have no problem accepting the idea that writing is a way to communicate with another person. If the ideas are to be successfully communicated, then they must be presented in a form that society understands. Errors stop the reader. Thus it is not a question whether children should be taught writing skills, but *when* these skills are taught. Ill-timed criticism and correction of errors can stop children's efforts in expressing ideas in written form more quickly than any other factor.

Two other important considerations must be taken into account in writing programs for gifted children. These are 1) teaching children *editing* skills rather than proofreading skills, and 2) providing readers (not including the teacher) with the red pencil for young writers.

Editing a written work *improves*, rather than corrects, the work. In teaching children to edit, the emphasis is on making the work better. If a word is misspelled, circling the word is no help, but spelling it correctly above the incorrect word *is* a help. If a statement is not clear when a child is editing the work of another child, the editor should rewrite the statement to show how the idea can be communicated more effectively. Once they have been taught the process, the best editors of gifted children's work are other gifted children. Editing each other's work provides young writers with readers, and the practice can be extended with publication of the work, perhaps as class or individual student books, newspaper articles, tape scripts that are recorded, plays that are presented, or poetry that is shared.

Encouraging creative expression of individual ideas among academically talented students is one of the most difficult tasks facing the teacher of writing. Teachers working with gifted classes for the first time are often surprised at students' use of stereotyped characters and situations, and amazed at the length of time it takes many of these students to produce an original composition. A partial explanation is found in the many research studies that show no relationship between high IQ and creativity. Since most children identified for participation in gifted programs are high-achievers, it follows that these students who do well on standardized achievement tests are convergent thinkers. In addition, many of these students are perfectionists and tend to be highly critical of their own work.

While the process of writing is a left-brain activity, the processes of visualizing, feeling, and creating are right-brain activities. The writer who has been told that the first paragraph or first page of a story must be perfect in order to hold the reader's attention tends to write, analyze, and rewrite that first page again and again, stopping the creative process before it begins. To keep ideas flowing, children must be encouraged to keep writing. Once the story is complete, then it can be edited for improvement. This process implies setting deadlines that, contrary to popular belief, often do stimulate the creative process.

GIFTED STUDENTS AND THE WRITING EXPERIENCE

Each summer at the Lindenwood Colleges in St. Charles, Missouri, gifted students between the ages of 11 through 15 gather for an intensive week-long writing experience. The following article describes this experience and the application of the approaches discussed here.

Gifted Students Write, Illustrate, and Publish All in a Week
(*St. Charles Post-Dispatch*,
Monday, July 20, 1981)

By Lia Nower of the *St. Charles Post*

Tea parties are not something young people often attend these days.

But Friday was a special day. And those attending were extraordinary people.

The youngsters were gifted students from elementary and junior high schools in St. Charles and St. Louis counties. They had spent the week at the Lindenwood Colleges under the tutelage of author David Melton, who taught them how to write, illustrate and publish their own books.

Friday was the final day of the week long workshop, so a tea was held for the children and their parents to display the finished works and explain the week's activities.

"Along with the books, the children were encouraged to do a lot of critical thinking, teaching them how to stretch their minds," said Nancy Polette, assistant professor of education at Lindenwood. "We required that the children be motivated to write or illustrate in order to enroll in the program, and we taught them to do a lot of cause and effect forecasting, which is what writers work from."

Ms. Polette who co-directed the workshop with Melton, said that between the two of them they presented the children with a variety of techniques and topics. She explained that, originally, the workshop was to include only 30 children, but 42 youngsters enrolled, and so Melton agreed to conduct two one-week workshops.

She said that deadlines were an important motivator in the project because "without deadlines, nothing happens."

Kathy Owens, an 11-year-old student from Progress South Elementary School in O'Fallon, said the workshop helped refine her skills.

"I really like to write and illustrate, and I would someday like to go into journalism at MU (University of Missouri at Columbia). So I came here to learn how to write better. When we got here, we did exercises to see how far along we were. Then we had a half hour to think of a story, and we took it home and finished it. The next day, we had it typed and started on the illustrations. It was really a neat experience."

Kathy's story, entitled "A Goddess Stands Guard," is about a girl who goes to Egypt and winds up in a King Tut mystery, she said. "I did lots and lots of research — I found out what was in the tomb, when it was found — it was a lot of fun to do the research, but it took a lot of time," she said.

Paul Wiley, 15, a 10th-grader at St. Charles West High School agreed:

"This week I think I stayed up until 2 in the morning every night. The deadlines really helped for the first part of the week, but they produced a lot of tension toward the end."

Paul said his father, Charles Wiley, is an English teacher and a good writer. And when Wiley noticed that Paul had writing talent, he looked for summer programs at Lindenwood and persuaded Paul to enroll.

"My book is about a king's son who doesn't like how his father tries to take over everyone else's land, and he finally overthrows him," Paul said. "The story has some magical elements like Tolkien uses in his books."

Paul's mother, Joyce Wiley, was amazed at her son's enthusiastic response to the workshop and the book he produced.

"His book was great!" she said. "In the beginning, the people in the story believed the world was flat but saw it was round when the prince restored peace in the end. I never knew he could write like that. Paul has always seemed like the kind of boy who could get burned out on school, but this week he has worked until 2 and 3 in the morning and only made one social call."

Nancy Bridges, whose 12-year-old daughter, Sarah, also participated in the program, explained that the free atmosphere of the workshop contributed to her daughter's appreciation.

"I think this week has been wonderful," she said. "Sarah's biggest complaint with school has been that they stress independence but make you line up for lunch, answer to a bell and so on. Here, the kids could leave the room when they wanted, arrange their desks like they wanted and literally be their own bosses."

Sarah explained that because her family moved to St. Charles from Switzerland in October, she enrolled too late to qualify for Coverdell Elementary's gifted-student program. But she feels that by participating in the workshop she will broaden her ability and polish her writing skills and increase her chances of being chosen for next year.

"I realy want to become a veterinarian, but I like writing," Sarah said. "One of my main problems is that I have trouble getting up the energy to get started, so when they tell me that I have to do this by a certain time, it really helps me."

She added that she will submit her story, which is about an orphan's search for freedom and identity, to *Ms Magazine's* "Stories for Free Children" section.

The writing modules that follow suggest numerous alternatives for stimulating the creative writing process, for challenging productive and critical thought, and for developing facility in communication skills. The modules cover a variety of topics and developmental levels. The reader is encouraged to select and adopt those that will best meet the needs of individual students or groups.

GIFTED LEARNING MODULE NO. 1:
Introducing Literary Style

In the study of literature, or in the development of creative writing, considerable attention is given to development of character, setting, plot, and theme with lesser attention given to the writer's style. Yet it is the development of a unique style that sets the writer apart and calls attention to his or her work. Children should be introduced to elements of style at an early age through the sharing of fine picture books. Older students will find picture books to be an ideal source for the study of literary style.

This module deals with the most common elements of style, encouraging students to examine picture books that contain these elements and to use a variety of these literary devices in their own work.

EXERCISES

Haven't We Met A'fore?

Independent Study
Literary Style for Young Writers

JULIUS SQUEEZER is:

a) a man who works in an orange juice factory
b) a python in the St. Louis Zoo
c) a play on words
d) all of the above

If you chose "all of the above" you're right! Words are an author's tools — to be added, subtracted, combined, twisted, turned and rhymed, taken apart and put back together again to create just the right idea or image for the reader.

Just as a carpenter's tools have names that indicate the use of each, the writer's tools also have names: alliteration, cliché, exaggeration, idiom, metaphor, onomatopoeia, oxymoron, parody, personification, pun, simile, symbolism, synonyms. These are just a few of the word tools that writers use and that you, too, can use. Get to know each one. Play with them in your own writing and be both delighted and surprised at the results!

I.   THE CLICHÉ (clee-shay)

Writers are often warned to avoid the **cliché** for these are words used so often they have lost their original meaning. However, if one really stops to think about the *literal* or actual meaning of the words in a **cliché** one cannot help but laugh. Can you really imagine someone "lending their ears" to you?

A. **Cliché**s are fun to play with. Find the **cliché**s in this story. Each has been given a little twist.

Midget Mouse, White House Reporter

Midget's home, office, and pressroom were located in the depths of an overstuffed chair in the Gold Room beneath the Oval Office, playing him, of course, at the seat of government. Accuracy and brevity were Midget's style, for one of the earliest lessons learned at his mother's knee was that "clarity begins at home." Midget's biggest scoop was the exposure of the hare-raising scheme of a janitor who was raising hares in the basement at the Pentagon. As the hares multiplied, the janitor's business scheme was exposed by the well-known hares' breath that filled every corner of the building.

B. Study the way Robert Kraus uses the **cliché** in these books:

Boris Bad Enough
Leo the Late Bloomer
Milton, the Early Riser
Pinchpenny Mouse
Noel the Coward.

C. Playing with **clichés** can be fun. Start with these.

Done to a turn could become _____
All's fair in love and war might be _____
A penny saved is _____
The bigger they come _____

II. EXAGGERATION

A. Tall tales are based on the idea of **exaggeration**.

Paul Bunyan had a pancake griddle so large he could skate on it. Pacos Bill traveled through a desert so hot and so dry that the rattlesnakes hid under the ground to keep from frying. John Henry won a race with a steam-powered drill by hammering so hard that he broke his heart.

Here are other examples of **exaggeration** by fifth-grade students:

"The sun was so hot it popped the corn in the field."
James Hall

"The wind was so strong it blew the paint off our car."
Michael Boxx

"The corn grew so tall only Martians could pick it."
Janet Smith

B. Note how author James Flora uses **exaggeration** in these delightful books:

Grandpa's Farm
Great Green Turkey Creek Monster
Stewed Goose

C. Try these for practice:

The skyscraper was so high _____
The rain fell so hard _____
The flower garden was so thick with roses _____

III. FIGURATIVE LANGUAGE

A. **Figurative language** can be fun to play with. Peggy Parish's *Amelia Bedelia* books use the *literal* interpretation of **figurative language** as the basis for their humor. Amelia Bedelia is a maid who follows her employer's instructions *exactly*. When told to "dust the furniture," she covers it with dusting powder. Imagine what she does when the note tells her to "draw the drapes"!

B.   Here is the beginning of a story using **figurative language**. Can you imagine what the literal (real) meaning of each sentence would be?

How to Relax

Do you have a lot on your mind?

Take a load off.

Get into the swing of things.

Take next week off.

Don't be a wet blanket.

Take forty winks whenever you need to and life will be a bowl of cherries once again.

C.   Watch for examples of **figurative language** in the books you read.

IV.   THE METAPHOR (met-uh-four)

A.   **Metaphor**s compare two or more things without using the words like or as. Sometimes a **metaphor** calls one thing by another's name or gives the qualities or actions of one thing to another.

Here are **metaphors** used by Lloyd Alexander in his book *The Truthful Harp.*

"A good truth is the purest gold and needs no guilding."

"Your tongue seems to gallop faster than your head can rein it."

Here are other **metaphors**:

"The snow was a white blanket on the ground."

"Abraham Lincoln was a giant of a man."

"The ship plowed through the sea."

B.   **Metaphors** are helpful in showing the reader exactly what the author means. Can you describe these topics through the use of **metaphors**?

The monkey
The old lion
Ebenezer Scrooge
The tall buildings
George Washington

C.   Other books by Lloyd Alexander that are rich in the use of **metaphor** include:

Coll and His White Pig
The Town Cats and Other Tales
Cat Who Wished to Be a Man

V.   ONOMATOPOEIA (ahn-uh-muh-tuh-PEE-uh)

    A.   What a beautiful word! It means using words similar to the sounds they make.

        Cannons CRASH, BANG, and BOOM.
        Tires SCREECH.
        Elephants CLUMP, CLUMP, CLUMP.
        Wolves HUFF and PUFF and blow houses down.
        Mud SQUISHES between toes.
        Potato chips CRUNCH.

        It is fun to use sound words in writing so that the reader can hear each sound just the way the author hears it.

        A silk skirt SWISHES.
        A boy with a sore throat GARGLES.
        A guitar string breaks with a loud TWANG.
        A balloon POPs, a gun BARKS, and so does a dog.
        An owl SCREECHES, a cat MEOWS, and a drum goes RAT-A-TAT-TAT.

        Using sound words to help the reader HEAR what you HEAR is using **onomatopoeia**.

    B.   Find and enjoy the following books by Peter Spier:

        Gobble, Growl, Grunt
        Crash, Bang, Boom

    C.   Reread a story you have written. How can you add *sound* to your story to make it more effective?

VI.   THE PARODY (pair-uh-dee)

    A.   A **parody** is an *imitation* of something that has been written, spoken, sung, or dramatized.

        George Mendoza has written a humorous **parody** on the song, "The Twelve Days of Christmas" called "A Wart Snake in a Fig Tree."

        Another **parody** on the same song reads:

        On the first day of Christmas my true love gave to me
        The money for a big shopping spree!
        On the second day of Christmas my true love gave to me
        Two winter storms and the money for a big shopping spree.
        On the third day of Christmas my true love gave to me
        Three snow shovels, two winter storms and the money for a big shopping spree.

    B.   Can you finish this parody? What else might be needed, given two winter storms and a lot of money to spend?

VII.   PERSONIFICATION (per-sahn-uh-fa-cay-shun)

    A.   **Personification** means giving HUMAN qualities to things or ideas, speaking of objects as if they were alive.

        Rudyard Kipling uses **personification** as well as **alliteration** in many of his stories. See what vivid word pictures he paints by using **personification** in these sentences from *The Jungle Book*.

        "All around the village the fields *lay* like aprons of patchwork on the *knees* of the mountain."

        "A few bands of clouds *raced* up and down the valley catching on the *shoulder* of the hills."

        "The wind *swept the floor clean*."

    B.   What words show **personification** in this sentence?

        "The rains gathered together for their last downpour of water fell in sheets that flayed the skin off the ground."

        See how clear the images are!

    C.   How might a summer storm have human qualities? Can you write a description of a summer storm using **personification**?

    D.   Enjoy these other books by Rudyard Kipling:
        How the Whale Got His Throat
        Just So Stories

VIII.   PUNS

    A.   Many words have double meanings. When they are used so that the reader is tricked into switching from one meaning to another they are called **puns**.

        Puns are found everywhere. During a bakery strike, a local newspaper printed recipes with this heading:

    BREAD EATERS MAY KNEAD THIS RECIPE

    Other punsters came up with these:

    EXPECTATIONS FOR BREAD SUPPLY RISE!
    NO TIME FOR SHOPPERS TO LOAF!
    BAKERS SAY, "NO MORE DOUGH, NO MORE BREAD!"

    Puns are fun and form the basis for many jokes and riddles.

    Question: "Why wouldn't the rattlesnake strike?"
    Answer: "Because it didn't belong to a union."

    Question: "How is a teacher like a candy stick?"
    Answer: "She likes to get her licks in."

    B.   Choose some word pairs to have **pun** fun with ... you might start with:

pain and pane	right and write
peel and peal	stare and stair
rain and reign	

C. For more fun with **puns,** see these books by Roy Doty:

Gunga, Your Din Din Is Ready
King Midas Has a Gilt Complex
Pinocchio Was Nosy
Puns, Gags, Quips, and Riddles

IX. THE SIMILE (sim-uh-lee)

A. A **simile** is used to compare two things by using the words "like" or "as." These **similes**

as big as a horse
as light as a feather
as clumsy as an ox

are used so much in our language that writers try to avoid them and use new **similes** to describe a person, place, or thing. If a "picture is worth a thousand words," the **simile,** like the **metaphor,** lets the author create such pictures in the mind's eye.

B. What pictures do these **similes** bring to your mind?

The ghost town looked like a picture of the end of the world.

The pink and white house on the hill stood like a birthday cake ready for a party.

The midget was as strong as 10 large men.

C. Poets often use **similes.** Examine several poetry books. What **similes** can you find?

D. Can you create original **similes** from these:

Frankenstein's monster was as ugly as _____

Vampire bats fly at night like _____

The haunted house was bathed in fog as thick as _____

X. SYMBOLISM

A. **Symbolism** occurs when one thing takes the place of another. The letters on this page are symbols that combine to make words that are written symbols of sounds you hear.

Many years ago Nathaniel Hawthorne wrote a story called *The Golden Touch.* It begins:

"Once upon a time there lived a very rich man and a king besides whose name was Midas."

The king could never acquire enough wealth to please him and was delighted to receive the gift of *The Golden Touch,* which turned into gold every object he could lay his hands upon. However, his delight lasted only until the moment he touched his beautiful daughter. She, too, turned to gold.

This story uses the symbol of the golden touch to represent greed and to show what happens when people decide that becoming wealthy is more important than anything else.

Many folk tales and myths contain **symbolism**. Read the American Indian story, *Little Burnt Face*. It is an even better story when you know that Little Burnt Face is the face of the hot, parched desert and that the Great Chief is the rain. These stories are much more fun to read when you look for the **symbolism** in them.

B.   List 10 common objects. Examine the properties of each. What might each symbolize:

    1.   _____flag_____ symbolizes <u>freedom, patriotism</u>

    2.   _____ symbolizes _____

    3.   _____ symbolizes _____

    4.   _____ symbolizes _____

    5.   _____ symbolizes _____

    6.   _____ symbolizes _____

    7.   _____ symbolizes _____

    8.   _____ symbolizes _____

    9.   _____ symbolizes _____

    10.   _____ symbolizes _____

XI. SYNONYMS

A.   **Synonyms** are words with similar meanings. They are among the most important of an author's tools. Without using a variety of rich, beautiful, exciting, and wonderful words, a story becomes DULL, DULL, DULL!

For example:

A monster might be big, large, great, king-sized, huge, gigantic, or massive. It could be found in a village, town, city, metropolis, or megalopolis. If you met such a monster and it were friendly, you might laugh, titter, snigger, snicker, guffaw, giggle, chuckle, or chortle. But if the monster were truly fierce, alarming, frightening, horrible, terrorizing, hostile, bellicose, belligerent, and unfriendly, help might be needed to chain, bind, restrain, fasten, shackle, or tether it.

Get the idea?

B.   Searching for the right word can be a marvelous treasure hunt. Select a favorite object to describe. Use a dictionary of synonyms or a thesaurus to add to your list of descriptive words. Write a description using as many of these words as possible.

XII. HACKNEYED EXPRESSIONS

A. In writing, expressions help the author to describe his thoughts. Some expressions have been used over and over until these expressions are **hackneyed expressions**.

Below are listed several **hackneyed expressions**. Across from these expressions rewrite these expressions. Be careful not to replace one **hackneyed expression** with another.

Hackneyed Expression	New Expression
After all is said and done	_____
Briny deep	_____
Iron constitution	_____
Last but not least	_____
Watery grave	_____
Poor but honest	_____
Nipped in the bud	_____
Easier said than done	_____
Better late than never	_____
All work and no play	_____

B. Look at your new expressions. Try using these in a sentence. You may try to write your sentences so that the sentences form a short story.

C. Read several newspaper or magazine articles on a topic of your choice. Bring to class examples of **hackneyed expressions** found in these articles. Be able to tell the class these **hackneyed expressions** and how you would change them to create a new expression.

BIBLIOGRAPHY

Alexander, Lloyd. *Cat Who Wished to Be a Man* (Dutton, 1973). *Coll and His White Pig* (Holt, Rinehart & Winston, 1976). *Town Cats and Other Tales* (Dutton, 1977). *Truthful Harp* (Holt, Rinehart & Winston, 1967).

Doty, Roy. *Gunga, Your Din Din Is Ready* (Doubleday, 1976). *King Midas Has a Gilt Complex* (Dutton, 1978). *Pinocchio Was Nosy* (Doubleday, 1977). *Puns, Gags, Quips, and Riddles* (Doubleday, 1974).

Flora, James. *Grandpa's Farm* (Harcourt Brace Jovanovich, 1965). *Great Green Turkey Monster* (Atheneum, 1976). *Stewed Goose* (Atheneum, 1973).

Kipling, Rudyard. *How the Whale Got His Throat* (Addisonian, 1971). *The Jungle Book* (Grosset & Dunlap, 1980). *Just So Stories* (Doubleday, 1972).

Kraus, Robert. *Boris Bad Enough* (Windmill, 1976). *Leo the Late Bloomer* (Windmill, 1971). *Milton, the Early Riser* (Dutton, 1972). *Noel the Coward* (Windmill, 1974). *Pinchpenny Mouse* (Windmill, 1974).

Olcott, Frances, ed. *Little Burnt Face* from *The Red Indian Fairy Book* (Houghton Mifflin, 1945).

Parish, Peggy. *Amelia Bedelia* (Harper & Row, 1963).

Spier, Peter. *Crash, Bang, Boom* (Doubleday, 1972). *Gobble, Growl, Grunt* (Doubleday, 1971).

GIFTED LEARNING MODULE NO. 2:
Stimulating Reading-Writing Skills

One of the best ways to stimulate writing activities is to expose children to writers who have both a unique style and a superb command of the English language.

Beatrix Potter combines a rare feeling for the best times of childhood with a rich use of descriptive language. While teachers tend to share her books with primary children, it is the upper elementary child who most often chooses Beatrix Potter titles for independent reading.

This module is designed to blend reading and writing activities and to stimulate creative and productive thought.

I. Fluency

    A. List as many furry things as you can.
    B. List all the things you can find in a barn.
    C. List all the animals that could live on a farm.
    D. List as many animals as you can that are main characters in stories.

II. Flexibility

    A. Categorize the furry things you listed (Fluency A.). How many categories do you have?
    B. How can we categorize the things you listed in Fluency B that you can find in a barn? How many groups do we have?
    C. Look at your list of animals from Fluency B. How could we group these animals?
    D. How can we group our list of uses of an egg? (Fluency D.).
    E. How can we put our animals in groups? How many groups do we have?

III. Originality

    A. What furry thing did you list that no one else did?
    B. What is the most unusual thing you think you could find in a barn?
    C. Make up an animal that would be well suited to live on a farm today.

D. Invent a new way to use an egg.

E. What animal characters did you list that no one else did? (Fluency B.).

IV. Elaboration

A. Choose one furry thing from your list. Make up a couplet about it.

B. How could you change one thing you could find in a barn today so it could be used on a space farm in the year A.D. 3000?

C. How could one of the animals on a farm today look in another 1,000 years if it were to adapt to life on a space farm?

D. Elaborate on one way you could use an egg if it were square.

E. How could you change one animal character so he could be a villain?

V. Planning

A. If I were to make a space farm, what materials would I need? Where might I build it? How would I build it? What problems might I have?

B. If I were to make appliances of eggshells, what kinds might I make? What else would I need? How would I put it together? What might go wrong?

VI. Forecasting

A. A farm for city dwellers to visit is being built across the block from you. How might this change your life?

B. If you wanted to have beehives in your backyard in the city, what problems might you have?

VII. Decision-making

A. If you could read books about only one kind of animal character, what kind would you choose? Are there many books about this kind of animal? Why do you like this animal species? What other considerations are there?

VIII. Problem-solving

A. You have decided to raise pigs in the city. Your neighbors are horrified and furious. What will you do? What else could you do? If you feel strongly about being on good terms with your neighbors, which is the best solution?

IX. Evaluation

A. If you could have only one kind of pet, what kind would you choose? Think of at least six choices. List the good points and the bad points of having each as a pet. Which one would your parents probably let you keep?

EXERCISES

I.   Peter's Downfall!

      Mr. McGregor did not like Peter Rabbit eating his fresh vegetables! He constantly chased and threatened Peter.

    A.   What other ways could he have kept Peter out of his garden?

          _____

          _____

    B.   Group these ways of keeping Peter out of the vegetable patch.

          _____

          _____

    C.   If you were Mr. McGregor, what way would you choose to keep Peter out? _____

          _____

    D.   Why did you choose it and not the others?

          _____

          _____

II.   Peter Rabbit Moves into Neighborhood!

      What might happen if Peter Rabbit were to move into your neighborhood? What might eventually happen to your neighbors' gardens, trees, and lawns? How might they feel about this? How could Peter's arrival change your family's life?

      Pretend you are a cartoonist. Make a cartoon strip below that will explain the changes in your neighborhood when Peter arrives.

III.   Peter Needs Help

      Peter Rabbit was desperate to get away from Mr. McGregor's garden! He asked the old mouse for help—but in vain. He almost asked the white cat for help, but he remembered Benjamin's narrow escape from it.

    A.   What other animals might he have met and asked for help in escaping?

    B.   Draw them and make a caption that tells how they could help him.

IV.   Put Peter on Film

      Peter Rabbit becomes outraged at having to mind his mother; he feels he is old enough and wise enough to be on his own. He decides to move in with his good friend Tom Kitten.

A. On acetate strips, use markers to create a filmstrip that shows what might happen when the two set off to explore the world.

B. Then below write the tape script to accompany the filmstrip.
Frame 1:_____
Frame 2:_____
Frame 3:_____
Frame 4:_____
Frame 5:_____
Frame 6:_____
Frame 7:_____
Frame 8:_____
Frame 9:_____
Frame 10: _____

V. New Uses for Old Things

Old Mrs. Rabbit, Peter's mother, discovers a new use for the herbs she mixes and sells!
You are a newspaper reporter. Write an article telling about Mrs. Rabbit's discovery. Also tell about her family's reaction to her new fame.

VI. Mr. McGregor's Rabbit-Proof Garden

You are Mr. McGregor and you plan to make a rabbit-proof vegetable patch. You are determined to have no more visits from Peter Rabbit and Benjamin Bunny!

A. Materials I need: _____
_____

B. I would make my garden (where): _____
_____

C. Steps in making the garden: _____
_____

D. Problems I might have: _____
_____

VII. Tom Kitten Goes to a Tea Party

One day Mrs. Tabitha Twitchit fetched her three kittens named Mittens, Moppet, and Tom Kitten to dress them for a tea party. Unwisely, she let them play outside in their best clothes until the company arrived.
They managed to give their clothes to the Puddle-Ducks. When their mother saw them, she was affronted by their state of undress. As punishment, they were sent to their room during the tea party — much to their delight!

A. Pretend you are Tom Kitten. How do you feel about wearing the uncomfortable clothes?
   1. I feel _____

   _____

B. What would our friends say if they saw you dressed up in your elegant clothes?
   1. They might say _____

   _____

C. What else could you do to get rid of your stiff, torn clothes?
   1. I could _____

   _____

VIII. Tom Kitten Goes to a Birthday Party

How could Tom Kitten dress to go to a birthday party in 1985? Make a slide show and narrative for five costumes he might wear.

NARRATIVE

Slide 1 — Tom Kitten is seen here wearing an up-to-date version of

Slide 2 — Here we see Tom Kitten wearing

Slide 3 —

Slide 4 —

Slide 5 —

IX. Trouble

Benjamin Bunny was quick to leap into trouble; he often acted without thinking of the results of his actions.

A. If you were Peter Rabbit, why would you follow Benjamin's reckless suggestions? _____

   _____

B. Why might you sometimes hesitate in following his actions — especially if he goes into Mr. McGregor's garden again?

   _____

   _____

C. As Benjamin's cousin, are there other things you should remember about him when he wants you to join him in mischief?

   _____

   _____

X.   Danger

Benjamin Bunny leads his cousin, Peter Rabbit, into a great deal of mischief and danger. Only the bravery of Benjamin's father, old Mr. Benjamin Bunny, can save their lives.

A. Can you think why these things happened to the rabbits?
CAUSE: Mr. Rabbit, Peter's father, was cooked in a pie by Mrs. McGregor.
RESULT: Peter's mother earned their living by knitting rabbit-wool mittens and muffetees.

B. CAUSE: Mrs. Rabbit needed more money.
RESULT: She sold herbs, rosemary tea, and rabbit tobacco (lavender).

C. CAUSE:_____
RESULT: Benjamin did not want to meet his aunt when he called for Peter.

D. CAUSE: _____
RESULT: Peter was not whipped by his uncle, old Mr. Benjamin Bunny.

XI.   The Foxy Gentleman Meets Old Mr. Benjamin Bunny

What might happen if old Mr. Benjamin Bunny were to try to rescue Benjamin Bunny from the foxy, whiskered gentleman? How might the two react to each other? What would Benjamin do during this time? How do you think he'd feel?

Write a story telling about the incident. Also make an illustration for your story.

XII.   Hide the Eggs

Jemima Puddle-Duck really wanted to keep her eggs to hatch into ducklings. She'd uselessly tried many times but they were always taken from her.

Help Jemima save her ducklings! Draw as many places as you can think of where she might hide her eggs.

XIII.   Egg Sitter

Jemima Puddle-Duck was a poor sitter for her eggs. Help her ducklings survive. Invent a new way she could keep her eggs safe and warm until they hatch.

A. How my egg-saver works_____

_____

B. Name of my egg-saver invention _____

_____

C. This is what my invention looks like:

XIV. Foxy Gentleman's Summer Home

What would be the most unusual thing you might find in the foxy gentleman's summer home among the foxgloves?_____

_____

A. Why would he have it?_____

_____

B. Name all the ways he could use it: _____

_____

C. How could you group these ways?_____

_____

XV. Jemima's Duckling

Jemima Puddle-Duck is a careless sitter. Suppose, however, one of her ducklings survives. Name all the words you can think of that would tell what her duckling would have to be like to survive:_____

_____

A. How can you group these descriptions? _____

_____

B. Now write the autobiography of her duckling. Tell how its personality and attributes have helped it survive under Jemima's careless supervision. _____

_____

XVI. The Foxy Gentleman

The foxy gentleman met the distressed Jemima Puddle-Duck and offered her the safety of his summer house among the foxgloves to hatch her ducklings. The simple Jemima never realized she was to be his dinner guest.

A. List all the words you can think of that would tell about the foxy gentleman: _____

_____

B. How could you group your descriptions of the gentleman? _____

_____

      C. Do you think Jemima or the foxy gentleman was the smarter one?

      _____

      _____

      D. Why do you think so?_____

      _____

XVII.   Presenting: Mrs. Tittlemouse Halts the Invaders

      Mrs. Tittlemouse doesn't want the insects and animals to sneak into her tunnels and nut cellar again!

      Write a script for a puppet play that tells how she keeps them out of her house. Tell what materials she uses to keep her home safe from the invaders. Also tell about any problems she might have to solve.

XVIII.   A Clutterproof Home

      A. Materials needed for a clutterproof home _____

      _____

      B. Where to build a clutterproof home _____

      _____

      C. Steps to follow to build a clutterproof home _____

      _____

      D. Problems to avoid _____

      _____

XIX.   Elaboration in Poetry

      Mrs. Thomasina Tittlemouse hid while the toothless Mr. Jackson pulled the bee nest out of her nut cellar. When she peeked out after he left, she was dismayed at the clutter and untidiness.

      A. Underline the important words in the paragraph below.

      B. The untidiness in the nut cellar was something dreadful—"Never did I see such a mess—smears of honey; and mess, and thistledown—and marks of big and little dirty feet—all over my nice clean house!"

      C. Now use the underlined words to make a poem about what Mrs. Tittlemouse saw. _____

      _____

      _____

XX.   Help

Mrs. Tittlemouse had to ask Mr. Jackson for help in getting rid of Babbity Bumble and his friends. Then she had to partly close her front door to get rid of Mr. Jackson.

Pretend you are a newspaper reporter. Write a report for your newspaper telling another way Mrs. Tittlemouse could have gotten rid of the bees. Tell why she chose this new method and the problems she had to solve.

XXI.   Mr. Jackson

Mrs. Thomasina Tittlemouse was very, very tidy. She kept her home spotlessly tidy. One day she found that Bibbity Bumble and other bees had made a nest in her nut cellar. She unhappily had to ask the frog, Mr. Jackson, to get rid of the bees.

A.   List as many words as you can that might tell about Mr. Jackson:

_____

_____

B.   Which of these words are good ways to be?_____

_____

C.   Which of these words are not good ways to be?_____

_____

D.   What other ways could we group these words that describe Mr. Jackson? _____

_____

XXII.   Television Reporter

Pretend you are a television reporter. You are assigned to interview Mr. Jackson and his bride, the former Mrs. Thomasina Tittlemouse. In your account below, tell how their marriage has changed both their lives — for better and for worse.

Good evening, friends, and welcome to the Jackson's home. Good evening, Mr. and Mrs. Jackson!

_____

_____

XXIII. What is the question, please?

A.   The answer is: BENJAMIN BUNNY
     The question is:

B.   The answer is: MRS. TITTLEMOUSE
     The question is:

C. The answer is: OLD MR. BENJAMIN BUNNY
The question is:

D. The answer is: MR. JACKSON
The question is:

E. The answer is: JEMIMA PUDDLE–DUCK
The question is:

F. The answer is: THE FOXY GENTLEMAN
The question is:

G. The answer is: MRS. TABITHA TWITCHIT
The question is:

XXIV. Characters from Beatrix Potter's Tales

A. Choose your favorite character from Beatrix Potter's tales. _____

B. Write all the adjectives you can think of that would tell about this character: _____
_____

C. How could you group these adjectives? _____
_____

D. Pretend the character has changed to be the opposite of the adjectives. Write a paragraph about how this character might act now in a story. _____
_____
_____
_____

XXV. Choose an Animal

A. If you could choose another kind of animal for Beatrix Potter to write about, what would you choose? _____
_____

B. Are there many kinds of books about this animal? _____
_____

C. Why do you like this kind of animal? _____
_____

D. What don't you like about this animal? _____
_____

E. Are there other things you should consider in choosing a new animal character for Miss Potter? _____
_____

BIBLIOGRAPHY

Potter, Beatrix. *The Tale of Benjamin Bunny* (Warne, 1904). *The Tale of Jemima Puddle-Duck* (Warne, 1908). *The Tale of Peter Rabbit* (Warne, 1903). *The Tale of Mrs. Tittlemouse* (Warne, 1910). *The Tale of Tom Kitten* (Warne, 1907).

GIFTED LEARNING MODULE NO. 3:
Starting with Prewriting Activities

Primary Writing Activities with
Robert McCloskey, Bill Peet, Mercer Mayer, and Others

The critical thinking skills of fluency, flexibility, originality, elaboration, planning, forecasting, decision-making, problem-solving, and evaluation are used in this module to lead the gifted kindergartener into creative writing. The books used in the activities for motivation and follow-up can be read independently by the gifted kindergarten child, or they may be read to the entire class by the teacher.

Depending on a student's fine motor skills, a teacher may want to provide space on a work sheet for the child's response, or else allow the child to record answers on his or her own paper. The teacher should use his or her knowledge of the student to determine which method would be most helpful to the child. In some cases, when a particular child's fine motor skills are very limited, an older student or a volunteer parent may be used as a recording secretary. When taking dictation, the person should not edit the child's ideas, but enter them exactly as the child dictates.

Warm-up activities are provided for oral practice. Most of these may be used as full class exercises. Try one any time you have a few minutes — first thing in the morning, just before going to recess, etc.

WARM-UP ACTIVITIES

I. Fluency
    A. List as many ways of "telling" a story as you can (including non-verbal methods — mime, murals, dance).
    B. Name as many "storytellers" as you can. Did you include the names of people who paint, conduct orchestras, report the news?

II.   Flexibility
      A.   Categorize your "storytellers." Can you now regroup them into new groups?

III. Originality
      A.   What way of storytelling did you list that no one else thought of?
      B.   Tell a new ending to a favorite story you have just read.

IV.   Elaboration
      A.   Write and illustrate a cartoon to tell the story of several Mother Goose characters.
      B.   Increase a phrase, one word at a time, to create a more descriptive phrase. (The house — The big house — The big gray house — etc.).

V.   Planning
      A.   If I were to set up a classroom library, how would I do it? List materials, steps, problems.
      B.   If we wanted an author to visit our class, how would we invite one here?

VI.   Forecasting
      A.   You have been a bit too noisy and your parents send you to your room with no television or stereo. What will you do? (See *Where the Wild Things Are* by Maurice Sendak.)
      B.   You go to the store to buy a juicy red apple, but the storekeeper plays a trick and gives you a green plastic one. You take it home and put it in your window to ripen, but it falls out of the window and hits an old woman on the head. She yells at a little boy because she thinks he threw something at her. What might happen next — and what might happen as a result of that? (See *Who's Got the Apples?* by Jan Loof.)

VII. Decision-Making
      A.   If you could help the librarian order three books by one author for the school library, what author would you select? Consider: Books you have enjoyed and who write them. Does your library have many books by the author? Are they often out on loan? Cost? Other considerations?

VIII. Problem-Solving
      A.   You have a new baby sister at your house. Suddenly everything that was *yours* seems to become *hers*. You don't feel very good about this situation. What will you do?

      State the basic problem.

      List as many solutions as you can. Decide what the solution should do. Select the best solution. (See *Peter's Chair* by Ezra Jack Keats.)

IX.   Evaluation
      A.   Evaluate a book you (teacher) have just read to the class with the class.

List all the good points of the book.

List all its bad points.

Will you recommend it to another teacher or student?

EXERCISES

I. Rabbits

Huge Harold by Bill Peet, *The Tale of Peter Rabbit* by Beatrix Potter, and *The Velveteen Rabbit* by Margery Williams are all about rabbits. They are alike in some ways, but very different in others. Below, list the ways the three rabbits are alike and the ways they are different.

Alike   **Different**
_____
_____
_____

Name some other stories about rabbits._____
_____

II. More Rabbits

Ask your classmates to give you more titles of stories about rabbits. Collect as many rabbit tales as you can. How many ways can you group the rabbit tales? Tales about tame rabbits, wild rabbits, talking rabbits—what other groups can you make?

III. What Is Pink?

After reading Christina Rossetti's poem "What Is Pink?" have the children fill in the blanks using their own ideas.

A. What is black? A _____ is black.
_____

B. What is brown? A _____ is brown.
_____

C. What is red? A _____ is red.
_____

D. What is green? A _____ is green.
_____

E. What is blue? A _____ is blue.
_____

Note to teacher: This activity can be turned into a colorful bulletin board to provide some visual help for those students who may be having color identification difficulties. Add more colors to complete the basic eight colors to be identified.

IV.   *Countdown to Christmas*
      by Bill Peet

It's 10 days until Christmas. How do you feel those last days before Christmas? Start with the tenth day and write about what you would be doing or feeling each day.

A.   Days to Christmas
     Ten _____
     Nine_____
     Eight _____
     Seven _____
     Six _____
     Five_____
     Four_____
     Three _____
     Two_____
     One _____

B.   Read Bill Peet's book to find out what Santa had to do just before Christmas.

V.   *What If ...?*
      by Joseph Low

Read the book *What If ...?* by Joseph Low, then write endings for these "what ifs."

A.   What if a hairy werewolf walked into your bathroom while you were brushing your teeth?_____
     _____

B.   What if you were at a picnic and a big, mean-looking dog snatched your hot dog off your plate?_____
     _____

C.   What if a long, spotted boa constrictor crawled into your bed to keep warm some wintry night?_____
     _____

D.   What if you were swimming and a huge, lonesome sea serpent wanted to join you?_____
     _____

     Can you make up your own "what if" below?
     What if _____
     _____

VI. *Whingdingdilly*
     by Bill Peet

In this book, Scamp becomes unhappy with being a dog. He wants to be something more important, like a horse. A witch named Zildy uses magic rhymes to turn Scamp into the Whingdingdilly. Scamp then has a camel hump, camel hind legs with zebra stripes, a zebra tail, and front feet and legs of an elephant, a giraffe neck with squarish brown spots, a rhinocerous nose, elephant ears, and reindeer antlers.

You are to make up your own mixed-up creature. Below, some body parts are listed to help you. You may leave out some of those parts or add some ideas of your own.

After you have described your animal, give your written description to a friend. Your friend is to read your description and draw what he thinks your creature looks like. Does it look the way you imagined it?

You and the person who made your drawing should select a name for this new story character.

A. Write your description on the lines below.
    The _____
    BODY _____
    FRONT LEGS _____
    HIND LEGS _____
    TAIL _____
    EARS _____
    NECK _____
    NOSE _____
    OTHER _____
    _____
    COLOR _____
    SOUNDS LIKE _____
    SMELLS LIKE _____
    EATS _____

B. After you have named your creature, you may want to write a story about it. You will also enjoy reading *The Whingdingdilly* by Bill Peet.

VII. Mother Goose Rhymes

Here are some Mother Goose rhymes that describe some familiar things in two or three lines.

THE MIST

A hill full, a hole full,
Yet you cannot catch a bowl full.

A STAR

Higher than a house, higher than a tree,
Oh, whatever can that be?

AN ICICLE

Lives in winter,
Dies in summer,
And grows with its roots upward.

DAFFODILS

Daffy-down-dilly has come to town,
In a yellow petticoat and a green gown.

Write a descriptive verse for an animal, a plant, or some other object of your own choice.

VIII. *Lisa Lou and the Yeller Belly Swamp*
by Mercer Mayer

You are a little girl crossing a very scary swamp in a rickety, old rowboat. Just as you go around a clump of cattails, the gnarled hand of the swamp witch reaches out to grab you. The witch says she will eat you and chew on your bones. In your boat you have an oar and a bundle of dirty clothes. How will you escape from the witch? Your only advantage is – the witch cannot see very well. List some ways you could get away.

_____

_____

Select the way you feel is best and write a paragraph about how you escaped. In *Lisa Lou* by Mercer Mayer, Lisa must escape from the Swamp Witch and three other unfriendly characters. Read this book to find how she tricks the Swamp Haunt, the Swamp Witch, the Gobblygook, and the Swamp Devil.

IX. *Hubert's Hair-Raising Adventure*
by Bill Peet

Complete these rhymes about Hubert after reading Bill Peet's book.

A. The elephant said –
Hubert, your mane is a mess.
It is time you combed it, you know.
There are birds at the top,
building a nest
And_____

B. The crocodile said –
Dear Hubert, I'd like to help you,
I really am sincere.
Come closer to my swamp, my friend,
And_____

C. The old bird said—
That new hairstyle will never do.
You look like a giant square.
I have some scissors, and I will be glad,
To _____

X. *Blueberries for Sal*
by Robert McCloskey

(For a wider variety of ideas, do this orally with class.) After
reading the story of Sal's experiences blueberry picking, think of things
about the book you liked and things you did not like. List the
responses. Try to get an equal number on each side. After reviewing
the responses, ask the children to write a review of the book; either
recommending it to a friend or class—or telling why it is not a good
book to read.

Things Liked   **Things Disliked**

_____
_____
_____

Will you recommend or not recommend this book? _____

XI. *Professor Wormbog in Search for the Zipperump-A-Zoo*
by Mercer Mayer

You are a mighty hunter who has been hired by the local zoo to
capture a Moss-backed Piliphantus Grizzlywog. This is such a strange
and rare creature that there is great disagreement as to where you will
find it. All you really know is that it is green, likes to eat limes and fish,
and it is fond of whistling like a canary.

A. Tell how you think this creature will look._____
_____

B. Where do you think you will find it?_____
_____

C. How will you capture it and bring it to the zoo?_____
_____

Now read *Professor Wormbog in Search for the Zipperump-A-
Zoo* by Mercer Mayer to find out how he tracks his beastie and if
he brings one home. You'll like the ending.

XII. *Jennifer and Josephine*
by Bill Peet

Girl
Alone, curious
Tasted, broke, slept
Ran, frightened from bears
Goldilocks

The poem above is a **cinquain**, a five-line verse. **Cinquains** do not rhyme, but they describe something or someone. The first line has one word, a noun (person, place, or thing). The second line has two words, adjectives (descriptive words). The third line has three words, verbs (action words). The fourth line has four words, words that show feelings. The fifth line has one word, a synonym for line one. After reading *Jennifer and Josephine*, write a **cinquain** about Jennifer and one about Josephine. The first and last lines are done for you.

Car   **Cat**

_____

_____

_____

Jennifer   **Josephine**

XIII.   *One Morning in Maine*
        by Robert McCloskey

After reading *One Morning in Maine*, think about what happened to Sal's tooth when she lost it while digging clams. How did Sal feel when she discovered her wiggly tooth wasn't in her mouth anymore? Could this have really happened? Has your first tooth come out yet? How did you feel? Who pulled it, or did you lose yours as Sal did? Sal wished for an ice cream cone. Did you make a wish? Write a short story about what happened when your first tooth came out. If you have not had a tooth come out yet, write about something you might wish for when it does; or write about a friend who has lost a tooth.

XIV.   *Huge Harold*
        by Bill Peet

You know from reading the story *Huge Harold* that Harold wins the trotter race at the fair and becomes a hero. You are a newspaper reporter, and it is your job to write a newspaper article telling about this great event. Remember to tell — who, what, when, where, and how in your article. Also prepare a large headline for your article.

Write your article on a piece of paper. On another piece of paper (unlined) draw a picture to go with your news item.

XV.   *A Special Trick*
        by Mercer Mayer

If you know the story of the sorcerer's apprentice, you might think twice before bothering anything belonging to a wizard, sorcerer, or magician. Or would you? Would your curiosity get you into a situation similar to the one the apprentice got into when he used the magic words he knew too little about? Would you cast a spell and then not know how to stop it? Write a paragraph telling what you would do if you found an old book of magic spells.

You will enjoy reading the story of a boy named Elroy and what happens to him in the magician's tent in the book *A Special Trick*.

XVI. *The Giant Jam Sandwich*
by John Vernon Lord and Janet Burroway

Your town is suddenly invaded by a giant swarm of wasps. People cannot have picnics, farmers and townspeople are driven inside, children cannot play outside—it's a catastrophe. A town meeting is called to decide on a solution to the problem. Pretend you are the mayor and help the people find a solution to the problem.

A. Tell what the problem is. _____
_____

B. List several solutions to the problem. _____
_____
_____

Select your best solution. Write a short paragraph explaining how you would go about ridding your town of the wasps.
When you are finished, you may want to read *The Giant Jam Sandwich*. The people of Itching Town solve their problem in a most creative way.

XVII. *Buford, the Little Bighorn*
by Bill Peet

The words below are words Bill Pett used in his story to describe Buford. Select at least six of these words, add words of your own, and write a short poem about Buford.

Words from the book about Buford

scrawny	bewildered
little	unsteady
runt	harmless
top heavy	star attraction
helpless	hero
burden to his friends	beginner
unhappy	skier
tottery	

Buford

_____
_____
_____

XVIII. *Henry Explores the Jungle*
by Mark Taylor

Your name is Henry, and you have set out to explore an exciting place. You take along some food, your dog Angus, and flags to mark your way so you will not get lost. Where will you explore? It must be near your home. Will anything exciting happen to you? Write a story about exploring the place you have chosen.

There are several books about Henry and Angus. *Henry Explores the Jungle* and *Henry Explores the Mountains* are two that you will certainly enjoy.

XIX.   *Lentil*
        by Robert McCloskey

After reading the book *Lentil*, write and perform a play about the story.

A. Read the book.
B. Pick out the names of the characters.
C. What are the settings of the story?
D. List the events of the story in order.
E. Write what each person would say in each part of the story (your script).
F. Select your cast, director, those in charge of scenery, those in charge of costumes, those in charge of sound effects.
G. Read the parts, adding sound effects and making changes.
H. Prepare scenery and collect necessary wardrobe.
I. Rehearse, rehearse, rehearse!
J. Present your play to your parents, teachers, or other classes.
K. Take your bows!

XX.   *Merle, the High-Flying Squirrel*
        by Bill Peet

After reading the story of Merle, pretend he manages to untangle the kite from the tree. He then takes off to fly on to new adventures in new places. Think of places Merle might go. Draw pictures of Merle flying to these new places; and at the bottom of each picture, tell what is happening in your picture. Choose a title for your story, make a cover, and have the teacher help you bind your story as a book. Then share your book with the class.

XXI.   *The Velveteen Rabbit*
        by Margery Williams

(After reading *The Velveteen Rabbit*) — This book ends with the boy not knowing that the wild rabbit he has seen is truly his old bunny.

Write a new ending for the story, pretending that the boy discovers that his old stuffed bunny has become a real, living rabbit. Tell what you think the boy would do, and how this would change the rabbit's life.

XXII.   *Farewell to Shady Glade*
         by Bill Peet

Pretend you are a small squirrel living in a quiet woods. One day the peacefulness of your home is disturbed by the horrible roaring, clanking, and chugging noises of monstrous machines. Smoke and dust fill the once blue sky as the machines clear away the trees and grass to make way for a new shopping center. You and the other animals and birds are terrified. What are you to do? You must leave this place quickly, but how? Tell in a few sentences where you would go and how you would get there.

In *Farewell to Shady Glade* some animals have a similar problem. Read this book to find out how they handle the situation.

XXIII.   *Time of Wonder*
         by Robert McCloskey

Teacher-directed class project

In *Time of Wonder* we get the chance to spend a summer on an island. Nature has so many special moments to wonder about that the summer is filled with adventure. Each season brings us things to look at and wonder about. Pick a season of the year and discuss some of the events that take place during that time. Wonder about them. You might choose fall—leaves turning color, birds migrating; spring—baby animals being born, new growth appearing everywhere; summer—insects buzzing, flowers blooming; winter—icicles on the eaves, the beauty of snowflakes. Which one you choose depends on you.

Paint or draw pictures of the wonders of the season you have chosen. Write a two- or three-sentence text for each picture. Photograph the pictures and make a tape recording of the text. Now you have a sound filmstrip to present to other classes.

Slides may be used, or you may have the photos prepared in filmstrip form.

XXIV.   Creepy Crawlers

Wilbur the pig, in E. B. White's *Charlotte's Web*, became friends with a friendly spider.

A.   Suppose Wilbur had a terrible fear of spiders. What could he do to overcome his problem with this friendly creature?
      1. _____
      2. _____
      3. _____

B.   Suppose that Charlotte was not a friendly spider, but a vicious spider that threatened Wilbur's life. What could Wilbur do to solve his problem?
      1. _____

2. _____

3. _____

BIBLIOGRAPHY

Keats, Ezra J. *Peter's Chair* (Harper & Row, 1967).

Loof, Jan. *Who's Got the Apples* (Random, 1972).

Lord, John. *The Giant Jam Sandwich* (Houghton Mifflin, 1973).

Low, Joseph. *What If ...?* (Atheneum, 1976).

Mayer, Mercer. *Lisa Lou and the Yeller Belly Swamp* (Parents, 1976). *Professor Wormbog in Search for the Zipperump-A-Zoo* (Golden Press, 1972). *A Special Trick* (Dial, 1970).

McCloskey, Robert. *Blueberries for Sal* (Viking, 1948). *Lentil* (Viking, 1940). *One Morning in Maine* (Viking, 1952). *Time of Wonder* (Viking, 1957).

Peet, Bill. *Buford, the Little Bighorn* (Houghton Mifflin, 1967). *Countdown to Christmas* (golden Gate, 1972). *Hubert's Hair-Raising Adventure* (Houghton Mifflin, 1971). *Huge Harold* (Houghton Mifflin, 1961). *Farwell to Shady Glade* (Houghton Mifflin, 1966). *Jennifer and Josephine* (Houghton Mifflin, 1967). *Merle, the High-Flying Squirrel* (Houghton Mifflin, 1963). *The Whingdingdilly* (Houghton Mifflin, 1970).

Potter, Beatrix. *Tale of Peter Rabbit* (Warne, 1951).

Sendak, Maurice. *Where the Wild Things Are* (Harper & Row, 1963).

Taylor, Mark. *Henry Explores the Jungle* (Atheneum, 1968). *Henry Explores the Mountains* (Atheneum, 1975).

White, E. B. *Charlotte's Web* (Harper & Row, 1952).

Williams, Margery. *The Velveteen Rabbit* (Doubleday, 1958).

GIFTED LEARNING MODULE NO. 4:
Going from Reader to Writer

Literature as a Springboard to Writing
(Grades 4-6)

The Hobbit by J. R. R. Tolkien (Houghton Mifflin, 1966).

I.   Fluency:
       A. List all adjectives, not mentioned in the story, you can think of to describe *The Hobbit*.
       B. List as many kinds of settings for a fairy tale as you can that would be appropriate for a troll.

II.   Flexibility:
      A.   Categorize all adjectives listed in Fluency A. about *The Hobbit*. What descriptive categories can you think of?
      B.   Categorize all settings that would be appropriate for a troll. How many different categories can you find?

III.   Originality:
      A.   Use adjectives you listed in Fluency A. to write your own paragraph to describe *The Hobbit*.
      B.   Choose one setting from Fluency B. and write a paragraph that creates a specific mood.

IV.   Elaboration:
      Study the form of a limerick.
      A.   Choose another setting from your list in Fluency B. and write a poem to describe the setting. The poem should be in limerick form.

V.   Planning:
      A.   If you were to research the setting of *Amahl and the Night Visitors*, where would you need to look? What kind of books are available? Are there any other sources besides books? What are the sources? The product of the research will be a newspaper interview of Amahl.
      B.   If you were to write your own fairy tale, are there special elements you would need to include in your story? Where would you need to look to find out? How would you go about finding the answer? The product of the research will be your original modern fairy tale using information from your research.

VI.   Forecasting:
      A.   What if the townspeople in *The Emperor's New Clothes* had told the truth, how would the tailor's life change? Write a story and be sure the townspeople tell the truth.

VII. Decision-Making:
      A.   In the tale "Dick Whittington" from *Fairy Tales of Long Ago*, edited by M. C. Carey, Dick is an orphan who finally makes it to London. After a few small jobs, he is finally taken in by Mr. Fitzwarren, a rich merchant. Dick gets along well with the family, but not with the cook who scolded him all day. What if you were Dick, would you stay with the Fitzwarren family?

      Consider:

         You had been poor and were an orphan.
         You could not stand being scolded by the cook.
         You did not know the city of London.
         You had always been on your own.

      After considering these facts and deciding what would be best, write a paragraph and describe your life as Dick.

VIII.   Problem-Solving:

    A.   Think of yourself as the fox in Aseop's fable *The Fox and the Grapes.* You have been trying all day to get the grapes. How could you go about getting the grapes?

        State the basic problem.

        List as many solutions as you can.

        Decide what you want the solution to do.

        Choose from your list the solution that will solve the problem the best.

IX.   Evaluation:

    A.   You are still the fox in *The Fox and the Grapes.* Pretend that you were able to get the grapes. List all the reasons that you should have gotten the grapes and all the reasons that you should have left the grapes alone. Pick your best reason and write a paragraph that illustrates you did the right thing.

EXERCISES

I.   The Tinder Box

After reading *The Tinder Box* by Hans Christian Andersen, list as many adjectives as you can that describe the setting, soldier, witch, the hollow tree, and the dogs.

A. Setting　　　　**B. Soldier**　　　　**C. Witch**

_____

_____

_____

D. Hollow Tree　　　**E. Dogs**

_____

_____

_____

    F.   Pick one of these categories and write a poem using the words in the list as descriptive words.

II.   Pack Rat

In the story *The Cricket in Times Square,* Tucker mouse is described as a scavenger whose nest is filled with everything from buttons to crumbs of food.

    A.   If you were a clever mouse, what kind of things would you collect?

1._____	6._____	11._____
2._____	7._____	12._____
3._____	8._____	13._____
4._____	9._____	14._____
5._____	10._____	15._____

B.   Now, think of something you could arrange or assemble with the items from your nest.
1.   What is your invention called?_____
2.   What is it used for?_____

III.   What Word

The best friend of every writer is a dictionary! It keeps the writer from overusing words and helps him or her to find better words to use in creating a character, setting, or mood. Below you will find a paragraph from Hans Christian Andersen's *The Little Mermaid.* Many of the descriptive words Andersen chose to describe the bottom of the sea have been left out. Find the most descriptive words you can to fill in the blanks. You may find your description is more vivid than Hans Christian Andersen's!

Now you must not think that on the bed of the ocean there is only white sand. No, the most fantastic _____ and _____ grow there, with _____ and _____ so supple they respond to the _____ movement of the water. All the _____ and _____ fish glide in and out among the _____ . In the very deepest part lies the palace of the Sea King. Its walls are made of _____ . The windows are of _____ . The roof consists of _____ . In front of the door are beautiful shells and in the center of each is a _____ .

IV.   What Would Happen If?

Read each of the following and give as many possible outcomes as you can. You will need to read these stories.

A.   What if:
Only the witch can strike the tinder box? *The Tinder Box*
1.   _____

B.   What If:
The magical fish does not come back when called by the fisherman? *The Fisherman and His Wife*
1.   _____
2.   _____

C.   What If:
Nobody told the emperor about his new clothes? *The Emperor's New Clothes*
1.   _____
2.   _____

D.   What If:
The ugly duckling had not become a beautiful swan? *The Ugly Duckling*
1.   _____
2.   _____

E. Take one of your "what if" endings from one of these fairy tales and write a modern story using your new ending. Be sure your modern story has the same message as the fairy tale.

V. Descriptive Poetry

Hans Christian Andersen wrote many wonderful fairy tales. After reading about Andersen, choose descriptive words from your reading. Use the words to write a poem about Andersen. There is a catch—you may not use any of these descriptive words from the reading. You will need to use words of your own.

VI. Fantastic Story

In Ronald Dahl's classic, *James and the Giant Peach*, James finds excitement with a giant peach that's produced by a tree growing in his yard. James experiences further adventure with the animated animals that reside inside the peach. Be sure to read this wonderful fantasy!

A. If you were able to raise an unusual plant or animal, what would it be? _____

B. Think about the advantages and disadvantages of sharing your extraordinary plant or animal with the public. List them.
   Advantages: 1. _____
                   2. _____
                   3. _____
   Disadvantages: 1. _____
                   2. _____
                   3. _____

VII. *The Fisherman and His Wife*

In *The Fisherman and His Wife*, the fisherman catches a magical fish. The fisherman can let the fish go or keep it. What decision would you make?

A. Consider:

   How would life change for the fisherman and his wife?
   Wouldn't the fish be happier in the sea?
   What good would a magical fish be?
   Where would they keep a magical fish?

B. After you have made a decision, write a paragraph to convince people that your decision was right.

_____
_____
_____

VIII.   The Reason Is ...

Remember that folk tales are imaginary writings of how certain things came to be in our real world.

Joyce Arkhurst has written a folk tale called *How Spider Got a Bald Head.* Read and enjoy!

Use your imagination to explain why some animals look or behave the way they do. Suggested ideas are:

1.   How the zebra got stripes.
2.   Why the skunk has an unpleasant odor.
3.   How the elephant got such a long trunk.
4.   Why the snake is not furry.
5.   Why the bird chirps.
6.   How the spider got eight legs.
7.   How the rabbit hops.
8.   Why the lizard is able to change color.
9.   Why the hyena laughs.
10.   How the fish got gills.

IX.   In Peter's Shoes

Peter was a young boy who lived in Russia with his grandfather. It was winter and Peter wanted to play in the woods. Grandfather told Peter he could not play in the woods then, as there were many hungry wolves lurking deep inside the forest. Peter ignored his grandfather's orders and proceeded to try and catch a wolf alone.

Read Disney's version of *Peter and the Wolf* to learn about Peter's adventures and the problems he faced.

A.   You are alone in the woods and come upon a hungry wolf. Your only equipment is a rope and a toy gun. What will you do?_____

_____

B.   Imagine walking alone through the woods on a winter day. Think about the pleasant and unpleasant sights and sounds you might experience. List them.

C.   If you decided to go exploring alone in the woods during a winter day, think about the items you would take and why. List them.

Pleasant sights   Pleasant sounds
_____   _____
_____   _____
_____   _____

Frightening sights   Frightening sounds
_____   _____
_____   _____
_____   _____

C. If you decided to go exploring alone in the woods during a winter day, think about the items you would take and why. List them.

_____
_____
_____

X.   If Your Middle Name Were Geppetto

There once was a kind, old man who was a carpenter. His name was Geppetto. He lived in a small house. Geppetto kept many pets, but he longed for human companionship. One day he carved a peppet that looked just like a real boy. He called the puppet Pinocchio. Geppetto wished the puppet was a real boy. A good fairy heard Geppetto's wish and gave life to the puppet.

Pinocchio by Walt Disney is a story about a puppet who came to life. Suppose Pinocchio turned out to be a bad boy who was only interested in evil. If you were Geppetto, what would you do to try to help Pinocchio become a better boy?

1. _____
2. _____

If you had the power to make something come to life, what would it be? _____

Think about the advantages and disadvantages of informing the public about your magical powers. List them.

Advantages	**Disadvantages**

What might be some problems you would encounter after making something come to life? What would the good points be about your creation?

Problems	**Good Points**

XI. Lessons from Aesop

A. Read Aesop's fable *The Leopard and the Fox*. See if you can write the meaning of this fable in one sentence._____
_____

B. Now that you know the meaning, how many ways does that fable apply to your life?

_____
_____
_____

C. Create your own fable that illustrates the meaning of *The Leopard and the Fox*. Be sure you do not copy Aesop's characters or what the leopard did.

XII.   More Aesop

The Shepherd Boy and the Wolf, an Aesop fable, means "Liars are not believed even when they tell the truth." Rewrite this in your own words. You will have to do research to find the appropriate words. Example: What is another word for liars?

A.   Your meaning:

_____

B.   After writing the meaning in new words, write a modern story that illustrates the message *The Shepherd Boy and the Wolf* conveys.

XIII.   Problem-Solving with Aesop

Suppose you are the farmer in Aesop's *The Goose with the Golden Eggs*. You grew more greedy every day. You would like to have as much gold as you can, as quickly as you can. The goose lays only one egg a day.

A.   State the facts leading to the problem. _____

_____

B.   What is the actual problem? State the problem two ways._____

_____

C.   List as many solutions to the problem as you can. _____

_____

D.   Select two of your solutions that you think are the best. Give the results to each solution.

Solution No. _____: _____

_____

Solution No. _____: _____

_____

E.   Which solution do you choose and why? _____

_____

XIV.   *The Hen and the Fox*

A.   Read Aesop's *The Hen and the Fox*. After you have read this fable, try to write the meaning in only one sentence.

_____

_____

B.   Now that you understand the meaning, pretend you are a reporter for the local television station. Interview the hen and write your story so that it could be aired on the news. You will have to do research on the process of interviewing.

XV.   A Norse Tale

Read "Why the Bear Is Stumpy-tailed" from *Popular Tales from the Norse* by Peter Christian Asbjornsen and Jorgen Moe. You are to rewrite this tale in play form. Be sure you research the play form, how to use characters, scenery, costumes, movement and also prepare a program for your class. You are to be the director.

XVI.   Pick a Tale

Here are several lists of words. Pick one word from each group to describe your own fairy tale setting.

A. **Town**	B. **Weather**	C. **Time**	D. **Objects and Places**
London	Rain	3:15 p.m.	Cars
Paris	Sunny	12:00 midnight	Painting
Madrid	Cold	5:00 a.m.	Parthenon
Hong Kong	Misty	8:00 p.m.	Coloseum
Washington, DC	Snowy	1:00 a.m.	Mosques
New Orleans	Humid	4:00 a.m.	Trumpet
Istanbul	Sleet	11:00 p.m.	Secret
Rome	Frost	1:00 p.m.	document
Athens	Flood	6:00 a.m.	Fans
			Bull fights

E.   After you have selected one word from each column, create a setting that describes the mood of your fairy tale. This description should be a paragraph.

XVII.   *Treasure Island*

Here is a paragraph from *Treasure Island* by Robert Louis Stevenson. Read the paragraph and use it as the middle of your original story. Be careful not to use any of the material from the book. You are on your own.

"Silver hobbled, grunted on his crutch; his nostrils stood out and quivered; he cursed like a madman when flies settled on his hot and shiny countenance; he plucked furiously at the line that held me to him and, from time to time, turned his eyes upon me with a deadly look. Certainly he took no pains to hide his thoughts; and certainly I read them like print. In the immediate nearness of the gold...."

XVIII. *Huckleberry Finn*

A.   In Mark Twain's *Huckleberry Finn*, Huck's father comes back, and Huck finds his father in Huck's room. Huck's father makes him read:

"I took up a book and began something about General Washington and the wars. When I'd read about a half a minute, he fetched the book a whack with his hand and knocked it across the house. He says:

"It's so. You can do it. I had my doubts when you told me. Now looky here; you stop that putting on frills." (from *Huckleberry Finn*).

B.   In your own words, explain why Huck's father felt as he did. You will need to read *Huckleberry Finn*.

_____

_____

_____

XIX.   *Huckleberry Finn*: Continued

After Huck escapes from his father, he decides to go down the Mississippi River. Jim is accused of killing Huck. Later Jim and Huck meet, and Jim asks Huck to let him come along or he will be punished for running away and for Huck's murder. List all the reasons you can that Huck should take Jim along and all the reasons that Huck should take Jim back to the Widow Douglas.

A.   **Reasons to let Jim   B.   Reasons to take Jim back
       come along   to the Widow Douglas**

_____

_____

_____

C.   Pretend you are Huck. Choose one of your reasons and write a convincing paragraph that lets the reader know how you feel about slavery in the United States, and also read *Huckleberry Finn*.

XX.   Create a Villain

Create a villain. Here are ideas to consider. Think of as many words, phrases, or names to fit under each category as you can.

A.   **Name   B.   Ways to Stop Hero   C.   Deeds of the Villain**

_____

_____

_____

D.   **Friends of the Villain   E.   Places the Villain Lives**

_____

_____

_____

F.   Choose your favorite one from each group and write below.

_____

_____

XXI. Dialogue

    A. Now that you have created your own villain (originality), write a dialogue between the villain and the hero. Be sure to include in the dialogue the villain's name, deeds, friends, and how the villain is trying to stop the hero.

Dialogue

_____
_____
_____
_____

    B. After you have written the dialogue, you and a friend present the dialogue as a play.

XXII. You Are the Author

    Look back at your villain. Check your choice for name, ways to stop hero, deeds of the villain, friends of the villain, and places the villain lives. You have the beginning of a story. Use this to create your own story. There is a catch—you must make the villain the hero at the end of your story. Also, your story should be illustrated by you. No magazine pictures, please.

BIBLIOGRAPHY

Andersen, Hans Christian. *Anderson's Fairy Tales* (Collins, 1975).

Arkhurst, Joyce. *Adventures of Spider* (Little, 1964).

Asbjornsen, Peter, and Jorgen Moe. *East of the Sun and West of the Moon* (Dover, 1970 [1888]).

Brown, Marcia. *Dick Wittington and His Cat* (Charles Scribner's Sons, 1950).

Dahl, Roald. *James and the Giant Peach* (Knopf, 1961).

Disney Productions. *Peter and the Wolf* and *Pinocchio* (Random, 1974).

Grimm Brothers. *Tales from Grimm* (Coward, 1936).

Selden, George. *Cricket in Times Square* (Ariel, 1960).

Stevenson, Robert Louis. *Treasure Island* (Collins, 1946).

Tolkien, J. R. R. *The Hobbit* (Houghton Mifflin, 1938).

Twain, Mark. *Adventures of Huckleberry Finn* (Harper & Row, 1884).

5   THE THIRD R: RESEARCH

RESEARCH SKILLS FOR THE GIFTED

In an age when the total accumulated knowledge of the world DOUBLES every generation, it is vitally important that students acquire skills that are essential in supporting or denying concepts through the use of a wide range of educational media.

The basic skills of research, which will be defined more completely in this section, are the skills of LOCATION, ACQUISITION, ORGANIZATION, RECORDING, COMMUNICATION, and EVALUATION.

Unfortunately, many students, including those in gifted programs, lack these basic independent study skills necessary for successful research projects. While there are numerous exceptional elementary library/media center programs in the nation's schools, there are also many schools with less than adequate programs, and, ironically, a number of school districts have cut back on their library/media services in order to establish gifted programs!

A survey of teacher education requirements in the United States indicates little training in effective use of library/media centers. Because of this lack of training, students in many classrooms have not been exposed to the most basic research skills, and it cannot be assumed that gifted students have acquired these skills on their own.

Before requiring research projects in gifted classes, it is important to ascertain the student's level of skill development. The overview of research and reference skills that follows is intended as a guide to determining those skills that need to be taught.

RESEARCH SKILLS FOR PRIMARY GRADES

Students in kindergarten through grade three are often neglected when consideration is given to development of the work/study skills program in the school. The prevailing opinion in many elementary schools is that the primary child's day is so filled with acquiring basic skills of reading and mathematics that there is little time for addition of other material to the primary curriculum. The point missed is that introducing primary research skills as early as the kindergarten years is not an addition to the curriculum, but a functional application of those skills included in the curriculum.

Simple research and reference skills *can* be acquired by primary students and should be introduced in a functional situation in the kindergarten program and developed throughout the elementary school years. Skills should be taught that primary students will use, and the teaching of any skill should be followed immediately by application of the skill by the student.

The Scope and Sequence Chart (Fig. 5-1) which follows will indicate the range of skills that should be acquired by primary students by the end of the third grade. Many students in gifted programs will be competent in these skills by grade two if given practice in using them.

Primary Skills

Figure 5-1
Scope and Sequence Chart for Teaching Primary Research Skills

Skill	Taught & Reinforced at Grade			
	K	**1**	**2**	**3**
Library Citizenship				
Developing a proper attitude toward the rights and property of others	X	X	X	X
To learn the care of books and other library materials	X	X	X	X
To develop purposeful study habits in the classroom and the media center	X	X	X	X
To stress the responsibility of the individual in a group situation	X	X	X	X
Library Use				
To acquire the view of the library as a place containing many carriers of knowledge	X	X	X	X
To learn the varied uses of these carriers of knowledge in practical situations		X	X	X
To accept the librarian as one who is willing and able to assist students with questions and problems	X	X	X	X
To learn the procedure for borrowing and returning materials	X	X	X	X
To learn the location of the types of materials found in the library			X	X
Parts of a Book				
To understand the terms "title," "author," "illustrator," and "publisher" and to locate these in a book			X	X
To understand the terms "title page," "contents," "glossary" and "index" and to be able to locate information in the book through use of the glossary, contents and index			X	X

Skill	Taught & Reinforced at Grade			
	K	**1**	**2**	**3**
Parts of a Book (cont'd)				
To understand the meaning of the term "copyright date" and the importance of this date to the research process				X
Locating Fiction				
To understand the meaning of the term "fiction"			X	X
To know how books of fiction are shelved in the library			X	X
To know how records, tapes, and filmstrips of favorite stories are housed in the library			X	X
To be able to locate a book of fiction if given the last name of the author			X	X
To understand that all of an author's fiction books will be found together in the library			X	X
Locating Nonfiction				
To be able to define the term "nonfiction"			X	X
To know that nonfiction books are shelved in number order			X	X
To understand the call number as the address of the book in the library			X	X
To be able to locate a book of nonfiction if given the title or subject and the Dewey number			X	X
Reference Books				
To understand the meaning and use of a dictionary (primary) or pictionary	X	X	X	X
To be able to locate an entry in a primary dictionary	X	X	X	X
To understand the parts of a primary dictionary entry	X	X	X	X
To understand the function of a set of primary encyclopedias		X	X	X
To be able to select the volume needed according to subject			X	X

(Figure continues on page 126)

Skill	Taught & Reinforced at Grade			
	K	**1**	**2**	**3**
Reference Books (cont'd)				
To be able to locate an entry in the encyclopedia and to search for and find a specific answer to a question			X	X
To be able to prepare a simple research report and to present information to the class	X	X	X	X

RESEARCH SKILLS IN THE INTERMEDIATE GRADES

No matter what skill is necessary for a student to acquire, certain basic guidelines must be uppermost in the minds of the teacher and the librarian if the skill is to be successfully mastered. Foremost is the premise that the student must have a need for the skill and must be given opportunity to apply the skill in a functional situation. This basic tenet for successful acquisition of skills is often overlooked and is possibly the greatest reason for the lack of success of many skills programs.

Gathering an entire class together and presenting a talk or film on the parts of a book or the Dewey Decimal System (or whatever the information may be that it is felt the students need) is an archaic practice that has little value in any modern learning program. It may be that large group instruction can at times be successful, but, for the student who has no need for a particular piece of information, the information itself is useless, and attempting to present it to an entire class is an exercise in futility. The successful road to acquisition of independent study skills lies in the student's need for an application of the skill. This cannot be overemphasized.

A second premise that must be kept in mind before a program of skill development can be initiated is that acquisition of any skill must involve the more important skills of critical thinking and independent judgment. Every step in the research process requires evaluation on the part of the student. To locate materials, the student must evaluate and choose among sources. To acquire specific knowledge, he or she must be able to distinguish the real from the fanciful, fact from opinion, and the significant from the less significant. The student must evaluate the information gained in light of his or her own experience and draw conclusions based on this evaluation. In organizing and recording information, he or she must develop a logical sequence of data or events, determining cause and effect as well as pertinent details. In preparing the presentation, the student must know the needs of the group to whom the presentation will be made, striving for a presentation that will keep the interest of the group. This functional approach that stresses independent judgment should be well established by the beginning of grade four and expanded throughout the elementary years. Assuming that students have gone through the primary skills program, the following list indicates those skills that should be stressed in grades four through six.

RESEARCH SKILLS FOR GRADES FOUR THROUGH SIX

I. **Independent Study Skills**

The following skills are introduced in grades three and four, reinforced in grades five and six, and should be used with facility by students in grade six and above.

A. Skills of Location
   1. The student will demonstrate his knowledge and use of alphabetical order by placing author cards in order by first, second, and third letter.

   2. The student will demonstrate his use of the call number by locating one or more books by call number.

   3. The student will demonstrate his understanding of the Dewey number by locating more than one book on the same subject with the same Dewey number.

   4. The student will be able to locate a specific topic in a book through use of the index.

   5. The student will demonstrate his knowledge of information found on a catalog card by circling items on the card as they are named.

   6. The student will recognize differences in title, author, and subject cards.

   7. The student will be able to demonstrate the use of the card catalog by locating a title, author, and subject card for three different books, copying down the call number and bibliographical information and locating the book or audiovisual item in the library.

   8. The student will demonstrate by use his understanding of the purpose of the following reference tools:

      General Encyclopedia
      Science Encyclopedia
      History Encyclopedia
      Standard Dictionary
      Geographical Dictionary
      Biographical Dictionary
      Thesaurus
      Atlas
      Almanac
      Abridged Reader's Guide

B. Skills of Acquisition
   1. The user will demonstrate ability to determine the purpose for reading or the purpose of the research activity by stating the purpose in writing.

2. The user will show ability to grasp main ideas by noting these ideas on a note card.

3. The user will show ability to locate details related to the main idea through outlining both main topics and subtopics.

4. The user will demonstrate skimming skills by locating one idea or concept within a large body of material.

5. The user will show an understanding of major topics and subtopics in an article by preparing an outline of such topics.

6. The user will show ability to follow the sequence of ideas or events through preparation of a storyboard.

7. The user will show ability to determine cause and effect through oral or visual presentation of a topic.

8. The user will demonstrate ability to differentiate fact from opinion by selecting factual material from material that is based on opinion.

9. The user will show ability to differentiate the significant from the less significant by selecting only main ideas from his outline or storyboard.

10. The user will show ability to differentiate the real from the fanciful in his selection of illustrative material to accompany a story or report.

11. The user will show ability to develop and/or follow directions.

12. The user will show ability to summarize research material.

C. Skills of Organization and Recording
   1. The user will demonstrate an understanding of a bibliography and will be able to prepare a bibliography.

   2. The user will show ability to take notes relevant to the subject matter by following correct note-taking procedures.

   3. The user will demonstrate spelling skills through use of correct spelling in papers and reports.

   4. The user will demonstrate ability to place facts in sequence by preparing a report or storyboard.

   5. The user will demonstrate ability to outline.

   6. The user will use interesting words.

   7. The user will demonstrate knowledge of grammar and sentence construction.

   8. The user will demonstrate ability to write a well-organized report.

   9. The user will demonstrate ability to evaluate the finished product through self-evaluation and through acceptance of valid points in the criticism of others.

D. The Research Process
   1. Students in grades four through six will be able to demonstrate their understanding and use of the basic research process when they can:
      a) State the research topic correctly in written form.
      b) List basic information already known about the topic.
      c) List questions to be answered about the topic.
      d) List sources to be consulted to locate information.
      e) Locate those sources listed.
      f) Acquire specific information from these sources.
      g) Take notes.
      h) Outline the information.
      i) Prepare an oral, written, or audiovisual presentation to communicate the information to others.

E. Skills of Communication
   1. The user will present an organized and sequential report.
   2. The user will use clear speech in speaking.
   3. The user will be able to present main points and details in order.
   4. The user will be able to answer questions on the subject.

It is important to keep in mind that he preceding lists of skills describe the basic tools the student must have to develop original solutions, conclusions, or products. If skills are to be acquired in functional situations, it may be necessary to structure initial independent study activities until such time as students gain confidence in pursuing knowledge on their own. One model that places emphasis on both process and product follows.

The Research Process: A Model

Basic research skills enable one to locate information quickly and easily for ANY purpose. Knowing the process can speed up the search!

Step One: Isolate the major topic or problem to be investigated.

Examples: Sources of teen income
Cost of car ownership
Rock Stars: Separating Fact from Fiction
Football heroes

Step Two: Define the topic or problem by asking the right questions. Use the journalist's time-honored method!

A. Who _____
B. What_____

C. When_____

D. Where _____

E. Why _____

F. How _____

G. What if or suppose that_____

H. Opinions _____

I. Conclusions _____

J. Creative Product:_____

Step Three: Where to look (sources)

Interviews_____   Encyclopedia_____

Card Catalog_____   Reference Books_____

Magazine(s) _____   Officials_____

_____   Organizations _____

Almanac _____   Other _____

Step Four: Determine a process

_Discover	_Compare	_Simulate	_Contrast
_Identify	_Construct	_Report	_Survey
_Locate	_Paint	_Experiment	_Editorialize
_List	_Interview	_Classify	_Recommend
_Debate	_Discuss	_Write	_Product
_Invent	_Compose	_Match	_Record
_Other			

Step Five: Determine a product

_Report	_Chart	_Diorama	_Play
_Story	_Diagram	_Map	_Invention
_Poem	_Model	_Mobile	_Game
_Letter	_Tape	_Questionnaire	_Bulletin brd.
_Panel	_Filmstrip	_Advertisement	_Other
_Newspaper	_Collection	_Teach a lesson	_____
_Graph	_Diary	_Cartoons	_____

Step Six:

Summary:

Topic:

Major Research Sources:

Basic Processes:

Expected Product:

Deadline:

Once basic independent study skill processes and tools have been acquired, the teacher of gifted students should strive to provide as much freedom as possible for each student to pursue his or her topic. This includes freedom from time restrictions and may require dialogue with teachers of other subjects to avoid as much "slots and bells" learning as possible. In addition, independent study presupposes that all students will not pursue the same activity at the same time. It is essential that the teacher expect the unexpected and both value and nurture self-direction and responsibility. Students should be discouraged from seeking the teacher's opinion along each step of the project and instead be encouraged to evaluate their own work critically. Finally, every effort should be made to provide a learning environment that is stimulating. This means that the school setting may not always be the best place for intensive investigation and that the teacher must ever seek community contacts to provide information and services to students that are not available in the school.

Each curriculum-related research module included in this section does allow for individual choice of topics, materials, and products. Activities within the modules extend students beyond mere gathering of facts to analyzing material and using it in new and creative ways.

GIFTED LEARNING MODULE NO. 1:
Studying the Four Seasons (Kindergarten)

These activities are designed as an extension of the usual preschool or kindergarten study of the four seasons. Included are activities pertaining to the weather and holidays.

Although developed for use with gifted children, many activities are suitable for all children at the preschool or kindergarten level.

Due to the grade level involved, many activities are oral, and the prepared lesson is to be used as a guide rather than a work sheet.

WARM-UP ACTIVITIES

I. Fluency
    A. List all the holidays you can think of.
    B. List as many signs or symbols of the four seasons as you can.
    C. How many weather words can you name?

II. Flexibility
    A. Group the holidays you named in ways that show they are alike.
    B. Group some of the signs and symbols with the holidays.
    C. Group the weather words with the holidays.

III.   Originality
    A. Have you thought of another holiday that we did not list? (Fluency A.) What is it?
    B. Think of a new way to dress a familiar holiday symbol—animal, plant, or human.

IV.   Elaboration
    A. Build on this "phrase"—"The pumpkin" example—"The *big* pumpkin." Keep adding one word at a time.
    B. Draw a silhouette of a snowman on the chalkboard. Ask children to draw what they want added to the snowman. One at a time.

V.   Planning
    A. Plan a summer vacation.
    B. If you had to plant a garden for your family, what would you do?

VI.   Forecasting
    A. What would happen if it snowed on the Fourth of July?
    B. You are a 10-foot Easter Bunny. What could have caused you to grow so tall? What effect will this have on your activities?

VII.   Decision-Making
    A. If you could pick only one outdoor activity that you could enjoy, what would it be?

    Consider:

        Can I do this in all seasons?

        Do I need/have the equipment to do it?

        Other considerations?

VIII.   Problem-Solving
    A. It is spring, and each day the temperature is different—one day very hot, the next rather cool. You want to be comfortable at school so you must choose your clothes carefully.

    What is the problem?

    List some solutions.

    Choose the best one.

IX.   Evaluation
    A. You are a snowman. List all the good things about being a snowman. List all the bad. Would you like to be a snowman?

EXERCISES

I.   Clothing

An orally directed activity.

A.   What are the names of some of the clothes you wear? Think of the things that you wear every day, on *special* days, when it is *cold*, when it is *hot*. Close your eyes and "look" into your closet and dresser. What do you see?

B.   Teacher may wish to have children cut out or draw the clothes named. Use these pictures or drawings in following flexibility activity.

C.   Use pictures or drawings from fluency activity in naming articles of clothing.

D.   Many of these clothes are alike in some ways. Find and compare the pictures of clothing. Group them in ways they are alike. Look at groups that are made. Do we know why we put the items (example sock and shoe) together? Rearrange the pictures and make new categories (groups).

Move toward groupings of seasonal wear for unit purpose.

II.   Seasons

A.   After reading *A Book of Seasons* by A. and M. Provenson, discuss the names given to the seasons. Autumn has another name that is more descriptive of the season. Fall—a good name because the leaves do fall.

B.   Create new names for winter, spring, and summer. Consider symbols and characteristics of each season.

C.   Using the three new names and the word fall, rewrite the poem:

>   Spring is showery, flowery, bowery.
>   Summer: hoppy, croppy, poppy.
>   Autumn: wheezy, sneezy, freezy.
>   Winter: slippy, drippy, nippy.
>   Author Unknown

Remember to consider seasonal symbols and characteristics.

III.   Weather

A.   Predict the weather conditions for (a specified time). Teacher will record predictions. _____

_____

B.   How do different weather conditions affect you? Plants in your yard? Squirrels and birds?

C. An oral activity to be used after reading *Where Does a Butterfly Go When It Rains?* by Alvin Tresselt.

Teacher reads statement with children supplying the ending.

1. When it rains, a butterfly goes _____.
2. On a snowy day, a cat _____.
3. Thunder makes me _____.
4. The strong wind caused the kite to _____.
5. On a breezy, warm day the flowers _____.
6. If the sun is very hot, frogs in a pond _____.
7. An ice storm made the trees in the forest _____.
8. Lightning caused _____.

IV. Choose a Season

A. Teacher-directed oral activity.

If you could chose one season to last through the entire year, what would it be?

You must think about—

the type clothing you like to wear,

the foods that you might like best,

the things you like to do, especially those that you do outdoors.

B. Are there other things to consider? Carefully make your decision.

C. State the reasons for your choice.

D. After making a final decision of which season you would like to have last all year, you were to tell your reasons for your decision. (Teacher has prepared several sheets of drawing paper with child's "defending" statements written on paper.) You are to illustrate a book that I have prepared with your reasons for selecting _____ (season chosen).

Consider the problems you may have completing your book.

How will you choose to work? You may work alone or with someone who has chosen the same season.

What materials do you need? Where can you get them?

Allow children to do some mental and oral planning after planning with teacher. Because of grade level involved, teacher will often need to read text of books so children respond with relevant illustration.

V.   An Oral Listing Activity

ς

A.   Name some foods we find in the supermarket more easily at certain times of the year.

_____

_____

B.   List reasons why these foods are seasonal.

_____

_____

C.   Categorize the foods listed in the preceding activity. (This is to be a teacher-directed activity. The food names could be written on sentence strip. As groups are made, words can be placed on bulletin board.)

D.   Identify each category.

E.   Can we make more categories? Did we include fruits, Christmas goodies, traditional cold weather items.

VI.   Animals and the Seasons

Present activity orally.

A.   By using the outline drawing of a tree and stream, show animals and birds at home. Choose one season to represent.

B.   Consider:

How should the tree look?

What would the animals and birds do at that time of year?

VII. Weather Tic-Tac-Toe

Complete any three items across, down, or diagonally.

What happens if ....?

It is raining.	The wind is blowing.	A warm sun is shining.
It is snowing.	There is a tornado.	It is lightning.
The temperature is 100°.	The lake is frozen.	It is 0°.

Answers should reflect thinking in terms of all living things as well as those nonliving. Example:

There is a tornado.

Houses are destroyed.

People lose homes.

Wild animals may die.

Trees have broken limbs.

VIII.   An Oral Activity to Implement Reverse Thinking

If you were going on a trip to the beach, you would probably want your swinsuit and sandals, maybe a raft or beach ball. It's warm at the beach, and you would need those things. Let's pretend, however, that you live in a part of the United States where it is winter and very cold. When you pack for your trip to the beach, you forget about the warm weather there and, instead of packing your swimsuit, you pack your snowsuit.

I'm going to read you a little story about just that. I'll stop when I want you to give me a word.

Remember — tell me a winter word!

I'm so excited. Today is the day I leave for Florida. I'll have a great time on the beaches. I'd better get packed. I need something to wear on my feet, I'll take my _____ . When I go down to splash in the waves I'll wear my _____ . I think I should take along my _____ for swimming. I might want my _____ if I go for a long walk. Well, that seems like everything. Oh, wait a minute. Where are my _____ ?

Sample responses: 1. snow boots
2. heavy coat
3. sled
4. ice skates
5. skis
6. mittens

IX.   Symbols of the Seasons

A. Consider the symbols and characteristics of each season. With these in mind, plan and draw a flag representing the four seasons.

B. Planning

Oral directions from teacher

1. What is to be done?

2. Are there problems you may have while working on your project?

3.   List your materials.

4.   Verbalize your ideas.

—Project completed as independently as possible.

X.   Seasonal Poetry

A.   Read the poem "Something Told the Wild Geese" to the children.

Brainstorm.

Ask—If you were a wild goose migrating south for the winter, what things might you see and do? Predict problems you will face. How would you feel at the beginning of the trip? At the end?

B.   Have children dictate a story concerning their responses to the questions. Each child will "write" his own book then illustrate his story.

C.   Follow-up with the book *Go with the Sun* by M. Schlein.

XI.   A Problem

Read to children:

Jeff and Keri hurry to eat breakfast and dress in their snowsuits, boots, and mittens. Outside, there is lots of new snow and the lake is frozen. It is a great day for sledding and skating. Keri runs to the lake carrying her skates. Jeff follows with his sled. Sledding is Jeff's favorite winter activity. He especially enjoys finding a "bump" that will send him flying into the air and then crashing back down onto the snow. Keri likes to pretend she is a skater in the Olympics. Whirling and gliding, she can "hear" the applause of her make-believe audience, which is actually a row of small trees.

On the hill, Jeff is getting ready to jump on the sled for another trip over that extra big bump in the snow he just discovered. Keri is beginning to practice making figure-eights. Suddenly a large brown and white dog comes running from a nearby farm house. As he runs near the lake he starts slipping on the steep bank. Rolling and tumbling, he falls onto the ice of the lake—then through the ice and into the cold, dark water.

The dog scrambles to get back onto the ice, but it is so thin that it breaks again and again.

Keri starts to rush toward the poor animal, but realizes quickly that she is too small to help by herself. Just as she turns to yell to Jeff for help, she sees him hit the "bump" with his sled, fly into the air, and crash back down very hard. Too hard. She hears Jeff cry, "Oh! My ankle!" Running to Jeff, she discovers he is not seriously injured; but his ankle is probably sprained and he cannot stand up.

What can Keri do now? —to help Jeff? —to help the dog?

What are the problems? _____

What solutions can you think of to help Keri?

Choose the best solution.

Why do you think it is best?

XII.   More Problems

To follow activity about Keri, Jeff, and the big dog.

The book *Henry Explores the Mountain* by Taylor is another story with more than one problem for our hero to solve. It's a real adventure that takes place in autumn. The children may enjoy hearing it.

After reading the book:

Name some other ways Henry could have solved his problems.

Decide if your way or Henry's way is better.

Why?

XIII.   Weather Feelings

Teacher orally presents situation.

It has snowed all day and night. Most streets are blocked with snow, sidewalks are slippery, the weatherman on television says more snow is on the way. Many people are unhappy because they feel snow is bad. Others say snow is good for all living things. Is snow bad or is it good?

Describe how you feel about snow and why you feel that way.

I like snow!   **I hate snow!**

Advantages   Disadvantages

_____
_____
_____

XIV.   Care Enough to Send *Your* Best!

Using a greeting card as a model, design a card for your class to send to each teacher in your school to celebrate the first day of summer.

Write an appropriate verse to put inside the card.

1. Decide on message and mood to be conveyed.

2. Select materials to be used.

3. Brainstorm—What characters and objects should be in the illustration?

4. Brainstorm—What key words need to appear in the verse?

5. After decisions are made, consider problems and solutions to complete the project. (Allow independence in actual making of cards.)

6. This activity is linked to preceding activity.

     How do we produce enough of this one card we have created to give one to each teacher in the building?

Orally ask—

A. What is the problem?

B. List some solutions.

C. Choose two of the best solutions.

     Tell what is good and bad about each solution.

D. Select best solution.

Now—mass produce

     This can lead, of course, to decision-making concerning division of labor, etc.

BIBLIOGRAPHY

Provenson, Alice. *A Book of Seasons* (Random, 1972).

Schlein, Miriam. *Go with the Sun* (Random, 1975).

Taylor, Mark. *Henry Explores the Mountain* (Atheneum, 1975).

Tresselt, Alvin. *Where Does the Butterfly Go When It Rains?* (Lothrop, 1962).

GIFTED LEARNING MODULE NO. 2:
Having Fun with Animals (Primary)

Having Fun with Animals is a collection of exercises stressing the thinking and research skills. These exercises are suitable for students in the primary grades. They are also ideal for gifted programs where thinking skills (such as productive thinking, communication, decision-making, planning, problem-solving, and evaluation) are stressed. The exercises deal with dinosaurs, modern animals, and storybook animals and are presented in a fun and exciting way.

When using individual exercises, the teacher will have to decide on the mode of communication to be used, based on the reading level of the children. The exercises can be done with the whole class, in small groups, independently through use of a tape recorder, or by writing the responses.

EXERCISES

I.   Animal Alphabet

A B C D E F G

ANTELOPE, BEAR, CHIMPANZEE

ALL THE WAY TO Y AND Z

WILL YOU PLAY THIS GAME WITH ME?

Think of an animal name for each letter of the alphabet. Work with a friend on this.

a_____	j_____	s_____
b_____	k_____	t_____
c_____	l_____	u_____
d_____	m_____	v_____
e_____	n_____	w_____
f_____	o_____	x_____
g_____	p_____	y_____
h_____	q_____	z_____
i_____	r_____	

Were you able to find 26 of them?

Is there one for x?

II.   An Unusual Discovery

    A.   A young Tyrannosaurus Rex was seen in the woods at the end of your street. What are the reasons that it could be alive today?

    B.   What happenings will go on in your neighborhood because of this discovery?

_____

_____

III.   Measure Dinosaurs????

You are a scientist living 200 million years ago. Your job is to measure all kinds of dinosaurs. How would you do this? (Remember 200 million years ago there were no rulers or yardsticks.)

    A.   What is the problem? Tell it in two ways.

_____

_____

    B.   List as many solutions to the problem as you can.
        1. _____
        2. _____
        3. _____
        4. _____

Use the back of the paper if you need more room.

    C.   Choose two of your solutions. Tell what might happen if you used these solutions.

Solution _____

_____

_____

Solution _____

_____

_____

    D.   Which solution will you choose? Why? _____

_____

IV.   Dinosaur Diorama

Plan and make a diorama showing dinosaurs.

I am going to make _____.

The materials I will need are _____

_____.

The steps I will take are _____

_____ .

Problems I might have are _____

_____ .

V.   Kraken?

Long, long ago, people believed there were sea monsters. One of the monsters they believed in was called the kraken. We are told it had 10 long arms and was bigger than a ship.

We know now that there is no such thing as a kraken. But if there really had been krakens, what would they have looked like?

Describe his size, color, shape, and more.

_____

_____

Does your kraken remind you of any animal that lives in the sea today? — If yes, what is it and why are you reminded of it?

_____

_____

VI.   Many Mammals

There are approximately 4,000 mammals, including man. Mammals are warm-blooded, have fur or hair, and the babies drink milk from their mothers.

Remembering these characteristics, think of as many mammals as you can. Work with two or three classmates.

_____	_____	_____
_____	_____	_____
_____	_____	
_____		

VII. A Wish!

A genie has just granted you a birthday wish. You may choose any animal, as long as it's a mammal, and trade places with it for one day. However, the day must be your birthday. What mammal would you choose? _____.

But your mother, being unaware of your wish, has planned a birthday party for you.

You must decide if you want the genie to grant you THE WISH!!

List the good things about   List the not so good things
this wish.   about this wish.

_____

_____

_____

_____

VIII.   Pretty?

Find a picture of an anteater in the encyclopedia. Look at its odd shape. It licks up ants, even termites, with his long, sticky tongue. It's not a very pretty animal.

How could we change the looks of the anteater so that seeing him is more pleasant to us?

_____
_____

Why did you make these particular changes?

_____
_____

IX.   Whales Extinct?

It is sad to say that whales may some day become *extinct*. If this happens, there will *never* be any more whales.

Just think about studying whales in school. It will be like studying dinosaurs. You will only see pictures, skeletons, and fossils of the whale. You will never see a live whale.

Each year many whales are killed to make oil out of their blubber. Man uses whale oil to make lipstick, paint, and soap. What can be done about this?

A.   What is causing the problem? Ask yourself Who, What, Where, and Why. _____
_____

B.   What is the problem? Tell the problem in more than one way.

_____
_____

C.   List as many solutions as you can to the problem.
a. _____
b. _____
c. _____
d. _____

D.   Choose the two above solutions that you think will work best. Tell what might happen if the solution were used.
Solution _____

_____
_____

Solution _____

_____
_____

E.   Which solution would you use? Why?

_____
_____

X.   Reptiles and Amphibians

Do you know the difference?

Reptile and amphibian each name a separate class of animals.

A reptile has scaly skin and lays hard-shelled eggs on land.

The word amphibian means two lives. An amphibian lives one way in water and another way on land. They lay their eggs, which are soft and have no shells, in water. The babies look like fish and breathe with gills. Their gills disappear when they grow up, and they live on land.

Remember the characteristics of a reptile and an amphibian, and list as many characteristics of each as you can.

Reptiles   **Amphibians**

_____
_____
_____

XI.   Evaluate Insects

Insects are all over the world — in jungles, woods, caves, mountains, ponds, and in your own backyard.

Think about the insects you have seen. Evaluate the need for having insects.

List the advantages of   List the disadvantages
having insects   of having insects

_____
_____
_____

XII.   Insect Riddles

She comes to your picnic,
Not welcome one bit.
She's followed by workers,
What insect is it?

_____

Were you able to answer the insect riddle?

Below are some names of insects. Choose three of them or three that you know and write a riddle describing it. Do not write in the answer. Give it to a friend to answer.

moth	grasshopper	wasp
butterfly	beetle	praying mantis
flea	lady bug	fly

A. _____
_____
_____
_____
_____

B. _____
_____
_____
_____
_____

C. _____
_____
_____
_____
_____

XIII.   Tic-Tac-Toe with Classes of Animals

Complete any three squares down, across, or diagonally.

Name 5 mammals.	Name 2 character-istics of amphibians.	Name 3 reptiles.
Name 2 character-istics of birds.	Name the 2 classes of animals that have gills.	Name 3 character-istics of mammals.
Name 3 amphibians.	Name 2 character-istics of reptiles.	Name 5 birds.

XIV.   Off to Venus

Remember the story of Noah and the Ark? Noah took every kind of animal and its mate on the ark with him to save the animals from the Great Flood.

Well, a flood isn't coming, but you and your family were chosen to begin a new community on Venus. You have packed your spaceship with everything necessary to live. There is one more thing you must do before you leave. There is room in the spaceship for five animals and their mates. You must choose the five animals that you think are the most important to have in your new space community.

What animals would you choose and why?

Choice 1. _____
_____

Choice 2. _____

_____

Choice 3. _____

_____

Choice 4. _____

_____

Choice 5. _____

_____

XV.   Tales about Tails

Tails are a very useful tool to many animals. Some animals hang by them. Some fight off enemies with them. Some use them for warmth. Others balance themselves with their tails. Some keep flies off themselves with them, and some use them to sound a warning.
List as many animals as you can that have tails.

_____
_____
_____

Think about how these animals use their tails. Now write a poem about animals and their tails.

_____
_____
_____
_____

XVI.   Create Plants

You have heard of a pussy willow plant. Doesn't that remind you of a pussycat? Of what animal does a dogwood tree remind you? List five animals. Now name a plant after each animal. Tell what each plant looks like. How should we take care of it? Does it in any way look like the animal after which you named it?

1. _____
2. _____
3. _____
4. _____
5. _____

_____
_____
_____

XVII.   Help Toad

Frog was not feeling well one day. He asked his good friend Toad to tell him a story. But Toad could not think of a story. So Toad walked, stood on his head, poured water on his head, and banged his head against the wall, but he still could not think of a story.

Please help Toad make up a story that Frog would enjoy hearing.

_____

_____

_____

To find out the *real* ending of this story, read *Frog and Toad Are Friends* by Arnold Lobel.

XVIII. A Beautiful Animal

In a burst of laughter and moonshine, Flutterby was born one fine and beautiful evening. As her silver-blue cacoon shimmered in the starlight, she unfurled her wings and whinnied at the crystal night.

Tell what kind of animal you think Flutterby is. What does she look like?

_____

_____

Do the other animals like her? Why or why not?

_____

_____

Read *Flutterby* by Stephen Cosgrove to find out what Flutterby really is.

BIBLIOGRAPHY

Cosgrove, Stephen. *Flutterby* (Creative Ed., 1978).

Lobel, Arnold. *Frog and Toad Are Friends* (Harper & Row, 1970).

GIFTED LEARNING MODULE NO. 3:
Learning about Community Helpers

EXERCISES

I.   Words, Words, Words

Think of as many words as you can to describe the following:

A. A Policeman

_____

_____

B. A Nurse

_____
_____

C. A Garbage Man

_____
_____

D. Choose one of the community helpers from the words, words, words activity, and write or tell a short story using all the words you listed to describe your character.

_____
_____
_____
_____

II.   What Do We Do—Now!

Share with your class the delightful story *Miss Nelson Is Missing* by Harry Allard and James Marshall.

A. Discuss problems children encountered when Viola Swamp appeared.

B. Now have children tell or write a story about a policeman, fireman, doctor, or any community helper who is missing.

III.   Think of a Caption

Find a picture of a worker (community helper) and another person (example: a doctor examining a child or a passenger paying a bus driver) and mount it on a large piece of paper. During the day, children may write anything they want on the paper about what is going on in the picture.

To stimulate ideas, ask children questions like ...

"What might the doctor be saying?"

"How would you feel if you were the little girl?"

"What will the man do next?"

At the end of the day, read the comments and captions with the class and discuss the ideas.

IV.   I'm Hungry

You own the only restaurant in town. The following helpers come for lunch, and they are *hungry*.

The problem is, you can only give them foods that begin with the same letter as that which begins their name.

Example: Nurse Nellie: noodles, nectarines, nuts.

Now it's your serve:

1. Policeman Paul: _____, _____, _____
2. Teacher Tillie: _____, _____, _____
3. Fireman Fred: _____, _____, _____
4. Baker Betty: _____, _____, _____
5. Doctor Dave: _____, _____, _____

V. Should You Take the Job?

You can be the substitute teacher in your classroom for one day—if you wish.

Will you take the job

Advantages   **Disadvantages**

_____
_____
_____

VI. The Mixed-Up Day

Pretend a tornado swirls through your town and sweeps up all community workers. They return to earth unharmed but in another location. The teacher lands in the police station and the policeman is now facing 25 children at school.

What might happen?

Example: The policeman arrests all naughty children; the teacher has the robbers writing 100 times "I will not take things that do not belong to me."

Now make up some of your own silly situations, using other community helpers.

VII. Find the Answer

Think of a possible answer to each of the following riddles.

A. I keep you looking very fine.
I trim your hair and also mine. _____

B. Come to me if you are sick.
I'll make your better very quick. _____

C. If you need a number just dial O.
I'll try not to be too slow. _____

     D. I drive the train over the track.
       I like to go forward, not back. _____

     E. If someone steals your new bike.
       I'll catch him before he takes a hike. _____

VIII. Curtain Up

     A. Read *Policeman Small* or *Cowboy Small* by Lois Lenski.

     B. Now plan how you can act out the everyday life of an interesting community helper.

     C. Decide if you need any "props," "costumes," or "customers."

     D. Be prepared to act for the class.

IX. Make a Book

     Let's make a picture book of community helpers.
     Your group can decide how you want your book to look and how you will make it.
     Answer these questions before you start.

     1. What are you going to make?

       _____

     2. What materials will you need?

       _____

     3. What will you need to do first, second, next, last?

       _____ _____

     4. What problems might occur?

       _____

X. True or False

     Answer each of these questions with either true or false. Be able to defend your answer.

     1. To be a teacher, you must be a woman. _____

     2. A fireman is always a man. _____

     3. You only go to a doctor when you are sick. _____

     Now make up at least two true or false sentences for your teacher to answer. She must be able to defend her answer.

XI.   How about You?

Some community helpers wear uniforms, hats, or badges. Sometimes these uniforms, hats, or badges tell something about their jobs.
Design a uniform, hat, or badge that tells something about you. Share your creation with the class.

XII.   Let's Make Puppets

Make two community helper puppets.

You will need:

Paper
Crayons
Scissors
Sticks or straws

After you have finished making your puppets, plan a puppet show for the class. What will your two puppet helpers be saying to each other?

XIII.   Tools of the Trade

A. Let's name as many kinds of tools or equipment that community workers use that you can think of.

_____
_____
_____

B. After completing fluency activity above, begin reading *Mike Mulligan and His Steam Shovel* by Virginia Lee Burton. Stop reading at the point where Mike realizes he is trapped in the basement. Ask children to think about what will happen next. What would be a good ending to the story?

XIV.   What Is It?

After sharing *Mike Mulligan and His Steam Shovel* by Virginia Lee Burton, ask children to imagine different uses for tools, equipment, vehicles, or one of their toys.
Ask them to draw a picture of their "new invention" and be ready to tell its use.

XV.   Career Scavenger Hunt

A. Mount a picture of a doctor, a teacher, or a grocer (or any three community helpers) on two large sheets of paper.

B. Divide the group into three teams: "Doctors," "Teachers," and "Grocers."

C. Give each team a stack of magazines and glue.

D. When you say "GO," they are to look through their magazines and find pictures related to their team name. (For example, with a picture of a doctor, you could put an ambulance or medicine.) When they have cut the pictures out, they should glue them on the large sheet of paper.

E. After 15 minutes, stop the activity. Count and see which team has glued the most pictures.

F. Allow the other teams to challenge any picture with which they do not agree.

The winning team must be able to defend their choices.

XVI.   Community Helpers at Our School

A. List all the different workers we have at our school.

_____

_____

B. Let's design an invitation to ask each of our school workers to visit our classroom. An invitation should include who, what, where, and when.

C. What are some ways we could get our invitations to our school helpers?

_____

_____

D. Decide which helper you would like to interview when they visit our classroom.

_____

_____

E. Plan questions you would like to ask the person you have chosen.

_____

_____

F. Interview the person you choose so that other members of the class can learn at least three things about this person or his job.

BIBLIOGRAPHY

Allard, Harry. *Miss Nelson Is Missing* (Houghton Mifflin, 1977).

Burton, Virginia Lee. *Mike Mulligan and His Steam Shovel* (Houghton Mifflin, 1967).

Lenski, Lois. *Cowboy Small* (Walck, 1949). *Policeman Small* (Walck, 1962).

GIFTED LEARNING MODULE NO. 4:
Building America

Warm-Up Activities........................ 153-154

Exercises 154-161

WARM-UP ACTIVITIES

I.   Fluency
      A.   List the means of transportation available to the colonists.
      B.   List the activities the colonists used for recreation.
      C.   List the work that could have been done by children.
      D.   You have decided to move West. Your wagon is small. What possessions will you take with you?

II.   Flexibility
      A.   Use the list of possessions you said you would take West and tell whether they should go inside or outside of the wagon.
      B.   In what ways could the colonists have used dirt?

III. Originality
      A.   You are a tree near the place where the Pilgrims landed. Tell your feelings and fears.
      B.   How would you escape from an Indian camp?

IV.   Elaboration
      A.   How could the colonists encourage more people to come to America?
      B.   Start with these two words: "The colonists ..." Each child will add one or two words (no more than two) to tell the story.

V.   Planning
      A.   You must catch a wild turkey for Thanksgiving dinner. How will you do it?
      B.   After you choose your land, in what order will you develop it? Remember, you have to live there, too.

VI.   Forecasting
      A.   A flood comes and washes away the colonists' village and the Indian village. What will these people do?
      B.   What would the colonists have done without the Indians' help?

VII. Decision-Making
      A.   If you had to choose whether to be an Indian or a colonist, which would you choose? Why?
      B.   You have a choice of settling anywhere in the New World. What place will you choose? Why?

VIII. Problem-Solving
    A. You have chosen a place to settle in the New World. Decide what problems you will have and how you will solve these problems.
    B. You have been keeping a record of all the ways the king's governor has been cheating the people out of their money. You leave the book on your table one day, and a friend of the governor happens to visit you. The friend takes your book to the governor. What will you do?
    C. Guidelines for problem-solving warm-up activities.
        1. State the basic problem.
        2. List as many possible solutions as you can.
        3. Decide what you want the solution to do (your goal).
        4. Choose the solution most likely to achieve this goal.

IX. Evaluation
    A. Justify the King of England's right to tax the colonists.
    B. Justify the colonists' right not to pay the tax to the king.

EXERCISES

I. I See a New Land!

    A. People came to America for many different reasons. List as many reasons as you can why people would want to come to America.

    B. Put these people who came to America for so many different reasons into groups that would be able to work well together.

II. Home, Sweet Home!

    A. Think of all the different items you would find inside a colonial home. List these items.

    B. Place these items in as many different groups as possible.

III. I Can't Believe My Eyes!

    A. You are a settler in colonial America. Due to a disturbance in the atmosphere, you suddenly find yourself in 1981. List all the things you will see that you have never seen before.

        _____

        _____

    B. Choose one item from your list that you would take back with you to colonial America. Tell how you would use it and how you would explain it to your family.

IV.   It's a Living!

   A.   People who came to America had many different skills or ways to earn a living. As you observe a typical colonial village, list the skills you might find.

   _____

   _____

   B.   Choose two of these skills. Predict how each skill will be used 20 years after your observation.

   _____

   _____

V.   Let's Get Together

   A.   What are some reasons that groups of people living in a strange land would want to form a larger group to include all small groups? List these reasons.

   _____

   _____

   B.   In what ways could this larger group be formed?

   _____

   _____

VI.   A Song of Thanks

   You are so thankful for the help the Indians have given you that you want to honor them. Compose a song that describes your feelings.

VII.   I Wonder ...?

   You are an Indian child. You have just seen a huge boat on the Great Water. You watch it closely as it comes nearer and finally stops. You watch as you see people getting off the boat. Write a story about what happens when you meet a child who came on the ship.

VIII.   You Have to See It to Believe It!

   A.   Since you have come to America, you have not been able to sell your new invention, although you believe it will be a great value to the colonists. Describe your invention and tell how it can be used.

   _____

   _____

   B.   Draw up an advertisement to put in the local newspaper to attract buyers for your invention.

   _____

   _____

IX.   Here's Johnny!

A.   You are a host of a television talk show. You have been given the opportunity, by means of a newly devised time machine, to interview any famous person from the colonial time. This person may have been living in any country.

B.   Which person will you choose?_____

C.   Why will you choose this person?_____
_____

D.   Prepare the questions you will ask this person. Give his/her responses to your questions.
_____
_____

E.   Have a friend help you dramatize your interview.

X.   Will We Survive the Winter?

A.   List as many problems as you can that the Pilgrims had to face the first year they lived in the New World.

1. _____
2. _____
3. _____
4. _____
5. _____
6. _____
7. _____
8. _____
9. _____
10. _____

B.   Choose one of these problems and draw a picture to illustrate it.

XI.   Our Town

A.   Using pictures and diagrams from books about colonial America, create a model of a typical village. Use this work sheet to help you plan your village.

1.   I am going to make _____
_____

2.   The things I will need are: _____
_____

3.   The steps I will take are: _____
_____

4. The problems I might have are: _____

_____

_____

XII.   Celebrate!

The Indians have been very helpful in showing your village how to grow new crops of food. As the harvest is going on, you decide to plan a way to show your gratitude and to also celebrate the harvest. I will have a _____.

The things I will need are: _____

_____

_____

The steps I will take are: _____

_____

_____

Problems I might have are: _____

_____

_____

XIII.   Here Comes Trouble!

Suppose you are a newspaper reporter during the time the colonists and the Indians are learning to live together. As you live among the people, you begin to see trouble coming. Write a newspaper story predicting what will happen between the Indians and the colonists within the next 100 years.

XIV.   Wagons, Ho!

As more and more people came to America, some began to move West. Make a chart to show reasons that caused this movement and the effects of this movement on the land and other people.

Reasons for moving West	Effects on people	Effects on land

XV.   To Tell or Not to Tell ...

You have overheard a group of men plotting to burn down the Indian village outside town. Just as you start to run away to tell the Indians, you step on a twig and the men capture you. They tell you that if you tell anyone what they said, they will hide you on a boat going to England.

Examine the Consequences

If you tell the Indians	If you keep quiet
_____	_____
_____	_____
_____	_____
_____	_____

XVI.   A Message for You, Sir

Suppose that the telegraph had already been invented before settlers came to the New World. Messages could be sent across the ocean, but they could not be longer than 10 words. Names of sender and receiver are free. Write the basic message you would send.

To: King James

I have made contact with the local Indian tribe. The chief, Powhatan, is king of this land. We must make friends with him quickly so he will help us survive.

John Smith

_____ _____ _____ _____ _____

_____ _____ _____ _____ _____

To: John Smith

I agree that you must make every effort to become friends with Powhatan. I am sending some royal clothing as a gift to this king. Please deliver them in my name.

King James

_____ _____ _____ _____ _____

_____ _____ _____ _____ _____

XVII.   No Strangers Allowed!!

"These new people must not be allowed to stay in our land," said Chief Powhatan. "They have cut down the trees and all the game has gone to another place. They have guns that kill with fire. They have built houses on our land. We must make them go — NOW!"

Perhaps the Indians felt this way about the settlers, but the settlers did not feel that they were doing anything wrong. They thought they had good reasons for what they were doing. See if you can identify the problems the Indians had because of the settlers. Problems of the Indians:

1. _____
2. _____
3. _____
4. _____

Put yourself in the place of the settler. Retell the story, giving your reasons for the things you have done.

XVIII. This Meeting Will Come to Order!

You have been selected chairman of the committee to form a new government in the colonies. You must work with all the different colonies and get them all together. How will you plan for the first meeting? Use this plan sheet for a guide.

I am planning a _____.

The things I need to do are: _____
_____

Steps I will take: _____
_____

Problems I might have: _____
_____

Possible solutions to the problem: _____
_____

XIX. Snowed In!

The Pilgrims have arrived safely in the New World. They are very happy and thankful to be in such a place. It begins to get cold very soon. The Pilgrims have not had time to prepare for winter. The snow begins to fall. What will they do?

To help you solve this problem, use the work sheet.

Try using these steps to solve the Pilgrims' problem of winter.

A. State the facts leading to the problem:

WHO is involved? _____

WHAT are the circumstances? _____

WHEN did it happen? _____

WHERE did it happen? _____

WHY did it happen? _____

B. What is the actual problem? _____
_____

C. State the problem in a different way. _____
_____

D.   List as many solutions as you can to the problem. _____

_____

_____

E.   Select one of the solutions, and tell what would probably happen as a result of that solution. _____

_____

F.   Do you think this is the best solution to the problem? If so, tell why. If not, which solution would be the best? Why? _____

_____

XX.   Do I Have to Go to School?

The colonists have much to do as they establish a new life. But they also have children. The children must be given an education. Who will teach them? When will they have time for school?

A.   State the problem in two different ways.

_____

_____

B.   List any problems that contribute to the major problem.

_____

_____

C.   List as many possible solutions to the problem as you can. Also, list the probable consequences of each solution.

Possible Solution   **Consequences**

_____

_____

_____

D.   Decide on one best solution. Tell why you think this is the best solution.

_____

_____

_____

XXI.   Check This Out!

The King of England has sent you to the colonies to check out the rumor that many of the settlers are unhappy with British laws. You must identify problem areas, give possible dangers if the problem is not solved, and give a possible solution to the king for each problem.

Problem   **Danger**   **Solution**

_____

_____

_____

XXII.   The Value of One Person

A.   Select a person who was very famous during the colonial period. What contributions did this person make that were most important?

_____
_____
_____

B.   Choose one contribution you have listed. What was the value of this contribution?

_____
_____
_____

XXIII.   Indians! Go West!!

We know that the settlers finally forced the Indians to move further west and leave the land that had always belonged to them. You be the judge. List all the reasons why the settlers were right to take the Indians' land, then list all the reasons why the settlers were wrong.

Right   **Wrong**

_____
_____
_____
_____

Now, make your judgment. Were the settlers right or wrong? Why?

_____
_____
_____

GIFTED LEARNING MODULE NO. 5:
Developing a World View
(For Middle and Upper Grades)

Many activities in this module are divergent in nature. However, students must be able to justify their responses, opinions, or conclusions with reliable data. Students should be encouraged to seek data from many sources and to verify data by checking additional sources.

Each student should keep a careful record of the research sources used so that, if challenged, he can provide the data that served as the basis for his conclusions.

EXERCISES

I.   A Tropical Island

All the people eat coconuts, pineapples, and bananas on a tropical island. The only time it rains is at night, and the children play all day in the many lakes. The children are enchanted at night by folk stories told by their grandfathers. However, there are no cars, movies, or televisions. You may live there if you like.

A.   List all the advantages of living on the tropical island.

_____

_____

B.   List all the disadvantages of living on the tropical island.

_____

_____

C.   Source used _____

_____

II.   Geographical Terms

There are many special terms that are used in geography or the study of the earth's crust. How many of these terms can you name?

A.   Terms

_____

_____

_____

Now that you have named some terms, be sure you know their meaning.

B.   Source used _____

_____

III.   World Hunger

Millions of people in Africa die every year, not only in the Sahara Desert, but also in the tropical jungles. Locate two sources that explain the causes of famine. How can these causes be eliminated?
To solve this problem, use the following steps:

A.   State the facts causing the problem:

_____

_____

_____

B. What is the problem? Try to state the problem in more than one way. _____

_____

_____

C. List as many solutions to the problem as you can. _____

_____

_____

D. Select two of the best solutions. What would happen as a result of these solutions?

Solution _____

_____

_____

Solution _____

_____

_____

E. Which solution would you choose and why? _____

_____

_____

F. Source used: _____

IV. New Ways versus Old

A. Locate at least one reference source on family customs in Dahomey. Read about the customs.

B. You are a young girl living in Dahomey who plans to marry a young man also living in Dahomey. He is a lawyer in Porto Novo. The young man also has an apartment there. You lived in a small village as a young girl; when you got older you moved to Porto Novo and became a nurse. There you lived with relatives.

In Porto Novo, you met this young man and fell in love. A marriage will soon take place. However, your parents wish you to be married with tribal traditions in the village. You want to be married in Porto Novo. How will you make a decision?

Where will you be married?

Consider:

Your wishes for a simple wedding.

Your parents wishes for a traditional tribal ceremony.

C. Source used: _____

V.   A Practical Problem

Your family has a small farm in the valley that usually has a good water supply from a river high in the mountains. One morning you get up and look out the window and notice that the river bed is dry. Your father has gone to town and taken all the tools to the blacksmith shop to be sharpened.

After breakfast you decide to hike up the mountain to see why the river has stopped. You go alone because your brother and sister are too young. When you get to the gorge, you see that there has been a rockslide.

You notice some old building supplies from the old mine. How could you use the following items to help you?

1.   Old post from the mine

2.   Old coal car

3.   Old pieces of tin

4.   Old pick

5.   Old hand shovel

6.   Rope that has been left in the dry mine

VI.   Communication

A.   Communicating with people in other parts of the world is very important in order to understand their ways of life. How many different ways to communicate with people can you name?

Ways to communicate:

_____
_____
_____

B.   Locate a recent book on communication. Skim through the book to find other means of communication to add to your list.

C.   Sources used: _____

VII.   Plant Life

Natural vegetation refers to the plants that are native or natural to certain areas. Many times there are specific terms to describe natural vegetation. Below you will be given the answers. You are to give the question.

A.   The answer is: *Bush.*
        What is the question? _____
        _____

B. The answer is: *Chaparral.*
    What is the question? _____
    _____

C. The answer is: *Prairie.*
    What is the question? _____
    _____

D. The answer is: *Selvas.*
    What is the question? _____
    _____

E. The answer is: *Taiga.*
    What is the question? _____
    _____

F. The answer is: *Monsoon rainforest.*
    What is the question? _____
    _____

G. Sources used: _____

VIII. Changes

For five years there was a drought in your section of the country. Many plants died as well as crops, and much wildlife moved away. What changes did this drought have on the following:

Food Supply	**Remaining Wildlife**	**Soil**

Sources used: _____
_____

IX. Communications — Originality

You have been discussing with a friend the qualities and resources that would be found in an ideal country. Your friend and you decide that you would like to persuade your friends to join you in a new country. Write a letter to your friends trying to persuade them to join you. You may want to research various countries to find out some of the qualities and resources of other countries.

X. Common Interests

Below are listed several countries around the world. Read the list of countries and then place these countries in groups. Give your reasons for the groups.

Countries

Spain	Mexico	Columbia
Italy	Brazil	Saudi Arabia
Norway	Viet Nam	Iraq
Germany	Canada	United States
Denmark	Soviet Union	

Group   **Group**   **Group**

_____

_____

_____

_____

Reasons   **Reasons**   **Reasons**

_____

_____

_____

_____

Sources used: _____

_____

XI.   Fuel for Thought!

A scientist has just discovered a fossil fuel that has been buried for millions of years. This newly discovered fossil fuel is better than coal because there is no air pollution. However, the fossil fuel is found in only one country. Only the scientist knows where the new fossil fuel is located.

A.   List all the advantages to telling the world about the new fossil fuel.

_____

_____

_____

B.   List all the disadvantages to telling the world about the new fossil fuel. _____

_____

_____

C.   Where can you read about fossil fuels? _____

XII.   Along the Shore

A.   There are many countries that have coasts on the Pacific Ocean. How many can you name?

Countries

_____
_____
_____
_____

Sources used: _____
_____

B. Now that you have named these countries, why are they important to the rest of the world?

Reasons

_____
_____
_____
_____

XIII.   Decision-Making

A. In a small Mexican village there lived a family with a daughter, Rosa, and a son, Pedro. Both mother and father had worked very hard on their small farm to have enough money to send Pedro to school. The mother had to take in sewing to help the family. After a trip to Mexico City, which took a week, Rosa learned that many young women are lawyers there. Rosa asked her father if she could go to school as Pedro did.

Pretend you are Rosa's father. What decision would you make? Will Rosa go to school?

Consider:

Is there enough money?

Can Rosa help the family more by sewing as her mother does?

What are the traditions in Mexico regarding education?

B. A current book or article on life in Mexico City is _____
_____

XIV.   Take a Trip

A. Bob, your best friend, has invited you to go with his family on a camping trip to Yellowstone National Park. Even though it is June and warm in your home town of Gulfport, Mississippi, it is still cool in Yellowstone. What items will you need to take?

Items

_____
_____
_____
_____

B. What would you expect to find in Yellowstone Park that you would not find in Gulfport? _____

_____

C. Sources used: _____

_____

XV. Find the Common Factor

Tokyo, London, New York, Paris, Madrid, Washington, DC, Bonn, Moscow, Peking, Rome, Barcelona, Mexico City, Perth, and Montreal. This is a list of important cities around the world. How could these cities be grouped? You may need to read about these cities in order to group them. There may be more than this number of groups. Give your reason for your grouping.

Groups   **Groups**   **Groups**

_____
_____
_____

Reasons   **Reasons**   **Reasons**

_____
_____
_____

Sources used: _____

_____

XVI. Urban versus Rural

Mr. and Mrs. Thompson and their children are moving to St. Louis, Missouri, from Ashdown, Arkansas. The Thompsons have lived on a farm all their life and for generations as well. Their children were raised on the farm. The children are Kevin, 6; Laura, 12; and Tony, 16. What changes will this move have on the following:

A. Kind of work Mr. Thompson does

_____
_____

B.   The family budget

_____
_____

C.   The activities of:

Kevin   **Laura**   **Tony**

_____
_____
_____

D.   Think again about the Thompson family. Why do you think the family moved from Ashdown, Arkansas, to St. Louis, Missouri?

Reasons for the family's move

_____
_____
_____

E.   Sources used: _____
_____

XVII.   Protecting the Environment

An oil well deep in the Gulf of Mexico has started to spill oil into the Gulf of Mexico. The oil reaches the shores of Texas where many people rely on fishing to make a living. Many experts have been called to help. However, after long discussions, this well cannot be stopped. It is the opinion of the scientist that the oil will have to continue to flow until there is no oil left in the well. What changes will this vast oil spill have on the following?

A.   Marine life along the Gulf

_____
_____
_____

B.   Waterfowl along the Gulf

_____
_____
_____

C.   Economy of Texas

_____
_____
_____

D. Economy of U.S.

_____
_____
_____

E. Other Birds in U.S.

_____
_____
_____

F. Sources used: _____
_____

XVIII. Africa

As a biologist, you have discovered a way to grow corn in the deserts. You have been asked to go to Africa to help stop starvation there. A large company has also asked you to work for them in the United States.

A. List all the advantages for going to Africa.

_____
_____
_____

B. List all the disadvantages for not going to Africa.

_____
_____
_____

XIX. Industrialization

A. List all the reasons that you believe make the United States a leading industrial nation.

Reasons

_____
_____
_____

B. List the reasons many foreign products are popular in the United States.

_____
_____
_____

C. Study your two lists. Can you make any predictions from them?

D. Sources used: _____
_____

XX.   Events

Here is a list of events. See if you can write the problem that led to these events; then also explain what effects this problem might have.

Events:

Presence of rich soil, plentiful grasslands, vast game herds

Europeans came to Africa

Europeans had better weapons than the Africans

Europeans claimed the tribal lands for their own

Problem: _____
_____
_____

Effects of the problem: _____
_____
_____

XXI.   A Choice to Make

In the next few months, your father will become the ambassador to Algeria. You are having a difficult time deciding if you will like to live in Algeria. Make a list of all the advantages and disadvantages of living in Algeria. If you do not know about the country of Algeria, research may help you in making your list.

A. Advantages to living in Algeria.
_____
_____
_____

B. Disadvantages to living in Algeria.
_____
_____
_____

C. Sources used: _____
_____

XXII.   Kenya

This morning you were awakened suddenly by the doorbell. You hurried to the door and saw a man from Western Union with a telegram. Ripping open the telegram, you saw that it was from Aunt Sophia who lives in Kenya.

The telegram read:

CAN'T WAIT TO SEE YOU COUNTRY BEAUTIFUL PLENTY TO DO.

Now you are filled with excitement and wonder. Try to write a paragraph that describes the country and activities that you will see and do when you visit Aunt Sophia in Kenya.

Paragraph:

_____
_____
_____
_____

Sources used: _____
_____

XXIII. Climate

Climate affects soil, plants, animals, and people. How does the climate of Southern Europe affect the daily life of people in these countries? Name as many different ways as you can.

Ways life affected by climate in Southern Europe:

_____
_____
_____

Sources used: _____
_____

XXIV. United Kingdom

Life in the various countries in Europe is different. Would you rather live in the United Kingdom or Poland? Give reasons that are positive and negative for both countries.

A. United Kingdom   Poland
   Yes   No   Yes   No

_____
_____
_____

B. Make a statement that describes the majority of your opinions or reasons.

_____
_____
_____

C. Name your best reason.

_____
_____

D. Sources used: _____
_____

XXV.   Giants of Europe

Some countries are extremely important to the entire world; other countries tend to be less important. To understand why countries become important, you will need to look for factors that cause countries to be important in the world.

Here is a list of European countries. Read about these countries and decide why the country is important. Put the reasons for the importance by the country.

Country	Reasons
France	_____
West Germany	_____
United Kingdom	_____
Italy	_____
Greece	_____
Turkey	_____

Sources used: _____

_____

XXVI.   Life in a Commune

A commune is made up of many villages. The work, equipment, and land are combined from many villages. Profits for the commune are shared by all people. This is a way of life in some countries in Eastern Asia. List all the ways that life might be different for you if you lived in a commune.

A.   Ways life would be different:

_____

_____

_____

B.   Sources used: _____

_____

XXVII.   Monsoon Season

The countries of Southeast Asia have a monsoon season each year. This year the monsoon season did not come at the right time in order for the crops to grow. Southeast Asia is heavily populated. What problems would you predict for the people of these areas?

A.   Food _____

_____

B.   Economics _____

_____

C.   Family life _____

_____

XXVIII.   Questions to Ask

There are special terms that apply only to Australia. The answer words are those special terms. Write a question that will fit these answer words.

A.   The answer is: *Aborigines.*
What is the question? _____

_____

B.   The answer is: *Polynesia.*
What is the question? _____

_____

C.   The answer is: *Rugby.*
What is the question? _____

_____

D.   The answer is: *Great Dividing Range.*
What is the question? _____

_____

E.   The answer is: *Maoris.*
What is the question? _____

_____

F.   The answer is: *Outback.*
What is the question? _____

_____

G.   The answer is: *Great Barrier Reef.*
What is the question? _____

_____

H.   Sources used: _____

_____

XXIX.   Danger Ahead!

You have been given a chance to explore the Amazon River in Brazil. List as many dangers that you might encounter as you can. How might you cope with each of the dangers?

A. Dangers

_____
_____
_____

B. Ways to cope

_____
_____
_____

C. Sources used: _____
_____

XXX.   Fate in Your Hands

On your trip through the Amazon River Valley, you discover a rare and endangered bird. There is another one of these birds in the Bronx Zoo. The one in the Bronx Zoo is male. The bird you discovered is female. Before coming to Brazil, there was a newspaper article that described the quest for a female bird of this rare species. You have a chance to let people know that you have seen this bird, or a chance to let the bird live in freedom. The bird's fate is up to you.

A. List all the advantages of reporting your find _____
_____
_____

B. List all the disadvantages of reporting your find _____
_____
_____

C. One good book about endangered wildlife is _____
_____

XXXI.   Barriers

A. Pretend you came to America in the early 1900s and did not speak or read English. You did not know anyone in the United States. Your family is waiting for you in Albania. Predict as many problems as you can that you might face.

Problems

_____
_____
_____

B. What groups of people in the United States are facing these same problems today?

    C.   What can you do to help?

    D.   Sources used: _____
_____

XXXII.   A National Flag

    A.   Think of all the different reasons a country might need a flag.

Reasons

_____
_____
_____

    B.   Now that you have thought of reasons that a country might need a flag, create a flag that will represent the country, and let the world know for what this new country stands. To create your flag, you will need to develop an original country. You may want to think about colors, symbols, size, and shape.

TITLE, AUTHOR, SUBJECT INDEX